On the Road with Will Rogers

10/10/08

On the Road with Will Rogers

Lance Brown

Biddle Publishing Co.

Cover and book design by Dan McKissack
Front cover photo of Lance Brown by Jim Ream
Back cover and prologue photos of Lance Brown by Jim Polaski
All Will Rogers photos used by permission of the Will Rogers Memorial, Claremore, OK.
Library of Congress Catalog Card Number 97-70649
ISBN 1-879418-25-8

For Booking Information Contact:
Lance Brown
1000 N. Lake Shore Drive #507
Chicago, Illinois 60611
(312) 943-8381
or (312) 961-6034
email: lance@willrogers.net
web site: www.willrogers.net

Published in the United States of America by
Biddle Publishing Company
P.O. Box 1305 #103
Brunswick, ME 04011
(207) 833-5016

for Mom

"I am out to see how America is living...I am meeting the 'Regular Bird'–the one that lives in his town; stays in his town; is proud of his town; he offers no apology for not having seen last year's Follies, or any other year's. I wanted to find out what he was thinking about."

–Will Rogers
Weekly Article, 1925

CONTENTS

FOREWORD

I first met Lance Brown in Claremore, Oklahoma, where he was to be the parade marshal for the Will Rogers Days festivities. I think that was in 1993. For several years, he had been doing his one-man show, "A Tribute to Will Rogers," that I had heard was very good but had never had the opportunity to see. Now over the years I have seen a number of one-man shows about my father, but nothing prepared me for Lance and his show. The way he presented Will Rogers was a refreshing new concept to me.

A few years later, when Lance told me he was writing a book, I thought, "Poor old Lance, he must be playing with a short deck," for there have been some thirty-five or forty books about my father and there just ain't nuthin' new. But as I read the manuscript, I saw that Lance was doing the same thing he did in his show—making Will Rogers a contemporary figure, someone who people of all ages can relate to.

Through the middle 1920s and the early 1930s, Dad spoke and wrote on just about every important event that happened. In this book, Lance sets the stage for many of those events, giving the attitude and thinking of the people at that time. Then, using a current situation, he shows how Dad's material is as true and applicable today as it was when he said and wrote it. Just as in his show, Lance does a masterful job of jumping from Lance Brown, the narrator, to Will Rogers, the humorous philosopher.

As an actor, humorist, singer, writer, and humanitarian himself, Lance has a unique connection to and understanding of Will Rogers. What my Dad did, his beliefs, and what he stood for comes through in the pages of this book. Lance brings out that the world of Will Rogers' years was different from the one we have today—not only in our technology, but in the way we think, in many of our values, in our attitudes, and in a good slice of our morality. No matter that situations change; human nature never does. We are still driven by the same emotions, regardless of the times.

Much of Dad's thinking and humor came from his early years in the Cherokee Nation, developed while he traveled and worked his way around the world when he was twenty, and matured during his many years spent in vaudeville. He traveled over most of the United States and parts of Europe, and he met and talked with countless people from every walk of life. From this he developed an extraordinary philosophy made up of good horse sense, personal responsibility, and a strong belief in people. Through Lance's performances, he has found that there is a hunger for this philosophy, not only amongst those people old enough to remember Will Rogers, but in many younger people as well. In his writing, as on the stage, Lance shows us the timelessness of Will Rogers' words.

I believe you will find in this book the reason why Will Rogers gained such universal popularity with his usually humorous, often pithy, and, on occasion, critical remarks. I think you will find it most interesting and enjoyable. For the Will Rogers you will meet is the guy I knew as "Dad," or "the Old Man," or "Pa Willie." Reading Lance Brown is as great as seeing and hearing him…of course, you will miss his rope tricks, his guitar, and his singing.

James B. Rogers

PROLOGUE

My earliest recollections of Will stem from a story that my father told about "the day Will Rogers came to town!" The town was Roswell, New Mexico. It was the place of my birth, but the incident happened some ten years before I was born. My father was attending the New Mexico Military Institute at the time, as was Will's son, Jim. One day Will Rogers and Will Rogers, Jr., showed up on a mission to play some polo with Jim. The Institute had the best polo facilities in the Southwest, and Will wanted to get together with the boys around his favorite sport, next to roping. Many of the town folk turned out just to get a look at Will Rogers—journalist, movie star and radio personality. But, according to my father, nothing special happened. He said, "Everybody had a good time and Will just seemed like a real regular fella."

It wasn't the last time Will was to visit Roswell. On subsequent visits his Daily Telegrams had comments like the following:

> *"You have heard of great preparatory schools where they turn out great football talent for the large universities. Well, right here in Roswell, N. M., the prettiest little city you ever saw, is situated the New Mexico Military Academy, and their kid polo teams are famous. It's the incubator for coming international polo.*[1]
>
> *"...finally found one of our boys here that we hadn't heard from in months. He has learned to play polo here, but hasn't learned to write. Asked him why we never hear from him. Said he had forgot our address."*[2]

As a father I can tell you that little has changed over the years.

Prologue

My father was in the oil business, which put him on the road a lot. When he was away, the rest of us would do a good bit of traveling ourselves. My mother was a great lover of nature, and she wanted her children to be exposed to its wonders. She would frequently pack us all up for sightseeing trips. We got some of the normal kid stuff like a trip to Disneyland in southern California. But most of the time we were out seeing the Great American West: the Painted Desert, the Petrified Forest, the Royal Gorge, Seven Falls, White Sands, the Grand Canyon, Sequoia National Forest, and, I think, every mountain in the State of Colorado. Mother took us to see nature on a grand scale, but she also had an eye for its little wonders. I recall her pulling the car over many times just to take us all a short way off the road on foot to a place where she could point out one lonesome, but particularly beautiful, desert flower. If I have any creativity or sensitivity now, I owe it all to my mother. Today, at eighty-two, she still inspires me.

I recall vividly the many trips we made in those days, especially the ones to Carlsbad. A little less than two hours' drive south of Roswell sits one of the seven natural wonders of the world–Carlsbad Caverns. We went there seven times while I was growing up. Will also had been there – on Mother's Day no less. I was delighted to find this account of his visit, not only because it captures his boyish sense of wonder, but also because it mentions mothers, flowers, and my father's line of work:

> *"Celebrating 'Mother's Day' by giving 'Ma' Rogers a vacation. Picked her a white desert flower and walked her for seven miles through the celebrated Carlsbad Caverns. I thought the biggest hole in the ground was when you were drilling for oil and struck a dry hole, but*

this is bigger than even that. It's just the Grand Canyon with a roof over it. Then, when you get inside it's got all the cathedrals of the world in it, with half of 'em hanging upside down.

"If a 'drunk' suddenly woke up in that great hall in there, he would think he had died and gone to heaven, for that's the nearest thing to his imagination of the place."[3]

Another of my mother's fabulous road trips took us to Claremore, Oklahoma. I was about twelve years old, that age when adults are bigger than life. We spent a whole day visiting the Will Rogers Memorial. On that day, the imprint of Will Rogers was seared permanently into my little brain's hard wiring. Will would be with me for the rest of my life. Naturally, with our parents loving him just as much as we kids did, Will became an integral part of our upbringing. Many of his little quotations were used to illustrate points and give life lessons. The earliest of these sayings I remember were things like, *"Everybody is ignorant, only on different subjects"*[4] or *"It's great to be great but it's greater to be human."*[5] But many years would pass before I would begin to understand fully the impact this man would have on my life.

Will waited patiently while I grew up. I tricked Denver University out of a degree in Fine Arts, served four years in the Navy, and spent another four years as a social worker in an institution for the mentally disabled. During this time I was married, fathered a son, Gabe, and then joined that ever-expanding club of divorced people. Gabe's mother and I joined a smaller club: those who remain friendly in order to raise a child as a team. It seems to have worked out all right. The boy is now a young man, running his own show, learning the hard stuff that only experience can teach—and he's still on speaking terms with his dad.

When I was the age my son is now, I did a little bit of everything. I washed dishes, drove heavy machinery, waited tables, did janitorial work, painted houses, was a foreman at a car wash, and even did a little farm labor. If Will could have seen me gasping for oxygen as I shoveled manure out of chicken barns in 100° heat, he probably would have laughed. Undoubtedly, he had some similar experiences during his early days, working on a livestock freighter that took him from Argentina to South Africa.

Lance Brown as Will Rogers

I was about thirty years old when I finally figured out that picking a guitar was about the best way I could avoid work and make a living at the same time. I started playing and singing in local nightspots and spent some time corrupting other people's guitar technique by teaching on the side. I kept company with musicians who were ten years my junior, every one of whom could outplay me with ease. It occurred to me that if I was going to compete in this business, I'd better learn how to tell some jokes. It was then that I developed the "Rubber Chicken" philosophy of guitar playing. That is, just about the time the audience starts suspecting you can't play very well, you pull out a rubber chicken, everybody laughs, and they let you play another song. This developed into a habit of writing my own silly songs and telling stories from the stage.

About 1981, I chased the love of my life to Chicago. Debra Leyva-Brown is a native Chicagoan of Italian stock who told me she would follow me anywhere in the world—as long as it was an hour's drive from her mother. (Actually, it was the fact that Debra had traveled around the world three times before I ever met her that most impressed me.) It turns out that my wife is my best friend, my mother-in-law is a peach, and I have an affection for Chicago that probably parallels Will's love of New York. Besides, nobody can cook like these Italians. Nobody!

While setting up shop in Chicago I noticed two things: (1) Musicians who could do a little acting made better money and kept better hours than those who just played music, and (2) My audiences were disappearing every winter. Eventually I got wise and started following them down to Arizona, where I spent a couple of winters annoying snowbirds around Phoenix and Tucson. In those storytelling and musical shows, I would occasionally drop a little "Rogerism" from my youth. Since these quips never failed to get a tremendous response, I started polling my audiences, asking them if they would like to see a show about

Will Rogers next season. Their response was very encouraging. With my marketing research done, I returned to Chicago in the spring of 1986 then immediately left for Claremore, Oklahoma, and the Will Rogers Memorial and Birthplace. In the tradition of a monk seeking acceptance into a monastery, I sat in awe of this wonderful place and waited until I could get an audience with the director at that time, Dr. Reba Collins. Dr. Collins was very gracious, and she gave me some valuable advice that got me off on the right foot. She suggested that, unlike other actors who maintain the Will Rogers character for the whole time they are on stage, I should consider going in and out of character. This would move the show from a nostalgic approach that would appeal mainly to people who were alive during Will's lifetime to one that would reach audiences of all ages. The goal was to carry the legacy of Will Rogers into the next generation. I added cowboy songs and Roaring Twenties music to provide a little relief from the spoken word and started the ongoing process of learning rope tricks. I found Will's classic movie *The Ropin' Fool* very instructive, although—I must admit—rather intimidating. His mastery is unmatched, even to this day. Along with his movies, all of the photographs and historical artifacts at the Memorial served to bring Will to life. As I read more extensively, watched all of his films, and listened to his radio broadcasts, I became completely absorbed in this man's remarkable story.

About this time I had a dream I will never forget. It was short and simple. I was again a twelve-year-old boy holding the hand of an older man as we walked across a field of high grass. My first thought was that he was an uncle or an older brother, but when I looked up, it was Will looking down, grinning at me with his hat on the back of his head. I was so startled I woke up. I tried to go back to sleep so I could catch up with him, but he was gone. Many would say such a dream was the natural result of being so saturated with my subject. They are probably right, but I like to think of it as an endorsement. With Will's go-ahead, I debuted the show in January of 1987. It has been rewritten three times since then and has been performed in every state in the union except Hawaii. I must say I have been more than lucky. Since hitching my star to Will Rogers, I have been blessed.

Lance Brown as Will Rogers

My continuing efforts found a new booster in the Memorial's next director, Mr. Joseph H. Carter. The first time I met Joe, he greeted me with a slap on the back and two cardboard boxes filled with books containing nearly every word Will ever uttered or wrote. Joe put all of his staff and archives at my disposal, and to this day, I make several research trips a year to Claremore to take advantage of the abundance of material there and to get my regular dose of Oklahoma hospitality.

Prologue

In 1995, the door was opened to writing this book. The Will Rogers Memorial Commission, Joe Carter, the Memorial Staff, and the Sarkeys Foundation developed a CD-ROM called "Presenting Will Rogers." This technology opened up a new world of possibilities. By entering keywords, one can search for specific topics from the over two million words of Will's writings. It is possible to quote from over four hours of radio broadcasts, see film clips from his movies, and view over twelve hundred photographs. This technology made it possible for me to cross-reference Will's comments on specific subjects throughout his career and to integrate them into coherent speeches. I deliver these speeches to the general public, students, and various professional organizations while placing emphasis on those groups' particular areas of interest. I had always been able to create such material in a more limited way, but this new technology expanded that capability a hundredfold. The wealth of material that resulted went far beyond the scope of a two-hour stage production and made the writing of this book inevitable.

You now know how I arrived at this humble endeavor. But the underlying *why* is more important. Will Rogers has much to say to us today. But I fear he may be dropping through the cracks of history. It is ironic that one of the most significant pioneers of all our major media, excepting television, is rarely—if ever—mentioned in our classrooms. Will Rogers was the most broadly read journalist of his day, universally recognized as having his finger on the pulse of America. He rose to the top of every other field of endeavor he entered, including theater, public speaking, radio, and motion pictures.

But beyond Will's celebrity, he was a very positive influence on his times. During a period when the country was under great stress, Will Rogers, through humor and reason, helped to heal wounds that otherwise might have divided the country. He built bridges between people. Although at times he could be highly opinionated, at the root of all of his observances and witticisms was a basic love of humanity and a hope for the future. He maintained a personal life that was unblemished by scandal and left no hard feelings in its wake. Although Will was not perfect, he did his best to live a full and honest life. My hope is that, through this book, a little bit of Will's example will be passed on to the next generation.

INTRODUCTION

"The reason a white man always got lost and an Indian didn't was because an Indian always looked back after he passed anything so he got a view of it from both sides. You see the white man just figures that all sides of a thing are the same. That's like a dumb guy with an argument, he don't think there can be any other side only his... You must never disagree with a man while you are facing him. Go around behind him. Look over his shoulder and get his viewpoint, then go back and face him and you will have a different idea."[1]

—Will Rogers
Weekly Article, 1932

In presenting this material, both in public performances and throughout this book, I am not trying to promote any particular political agenda. Instead, I encourage a form of "Radical Middle of the Roadism" in which any viewpoint deserves both consideration and close scrutiny. Just as Will suggested in explaining why an Indian never gets lost, perhaps we should try to see the other person's point of view.

People often ask me questions like, "What would Will say about the crime situation today?" "What about our foreign policy?" "What would he think of today's politicians?" No one knows precisely what Will might have said about these things, especially on topics that were not of concern in his day. (Will had nothing to say about in vitro fertilization.) But I can approximate his responses by making my answers adhere as closely as possible to the exact words Will used relative to the issues that he did address. I never tamper with the meaning of Will's statements. But at times I add minor phrases of my own to smooth transitions. I also alter some of Will's written comments so that they are more easily spoken. Some of his longer speeches and articles have been condensed to more manageable sizes. But Will's core meaning and purpose are always left intact, as are all of his characteristic grammar and spelling errors. Will was often in a hurry. In places where his clarity really suffers, I have added a period or a comma so that the reader will not have to reread to get his meaning. Will's books and newspaper articles are full of deliberate little errors that contribute to his style. These remain. Early editors of Will's columns had to be told to stop correcting his spelling and grammar because they were destroying his homespun appeal.

The speeches that fill this book have been constructed from comments Will made throughout his career from as early as 1905 until the time of his death in 1935. The sources include Will's vaudeville and stage work, newspaper columns, movies, radio broadcasts, excerpts from his six books, and casual comments that were overheard by loved ones, close friends, and acquaintances. The comments are not in chronological order. For example, a statement made in 1933 may be followed by another made in 1927. Although the comments were made years apart and in reverse chronology, they still make sense when spoken together.

Will said some things you may agree with and others you won't. You may feel he would have changed his mind on certain issues today. We live in a world very different from what it was over sixty years ago. The truth is, there were times when Will was right on the money and other times when he totally missed the mark. A good example comes from a Daily Telegram he wrote on August 2, 1932, which read: *"Don't let Brisbane or anybody else who is going to fight the whole next war entirely with planes and poison gas do away with the cavalry. There is certain things you can't replace the horse in, and war is one of 'em."*[3] Will, above all, would have enjoyed a big laugh over just how far off he was on that one.

At times Will came down strongly on one side or the other of some of today's hot issues. Do the changes in our society negate Will's viewpoint or reinforce it? I present Will's words in the context of his times. You are free to interpret their relevance to our world today.

I hope you enjoy reading the wit and wisdom of this great American humorist as much as I have enjoyed preparing and presenting it. The more you read and learn about this man, the more hope and humor you may have about life in general. You will probably find Will's wit, optimism, and love of humanity quite contagious. I know I do.

On the Road with Will Rogers

1

WILL ROGERS—LIFE AND TIMES

William Penn Adair Rogers was born November 4, 1879, just outside a little settlement called Oologah, in what was then Indian Territory and is now the state of Oklahoma. At that time, Oologah was very small, amounting to just a few buildings. It was not officially established as a township until 1890. As Will grew up, his father's business moved into nearby Claremore, which Will always claimed as his home town.

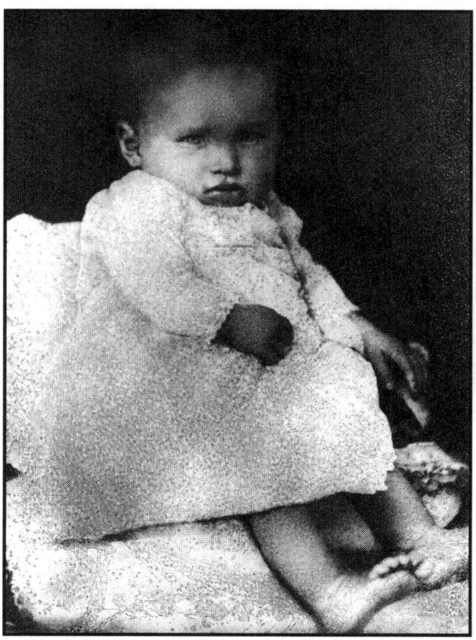

Will Rogers

Born just fourteen years after the end of the Civil War, Will entered a world where many of the physical and emotional scars of that conflict were still in evidence. Will's father, Clem Vann Rogers, had fought on the side of the Confederacy, as did many land-owning people of Indian extraction. Will claimed that his father was one eighth Cherokee Indian and his mother, Mary Schrimsher Rogers, was one quarter blood. But the official tribal records list Will as nine thirty-seconds. He said, *"I have just enough white blood in me to make my honesty questionable."*[1]

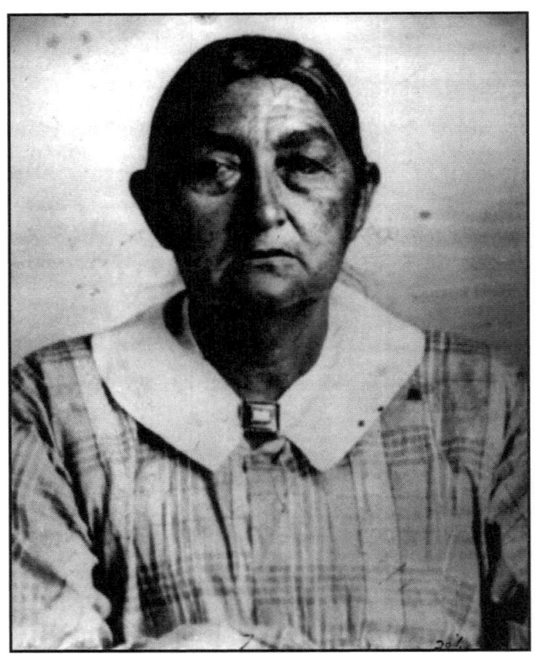

Will's maternal grandmother–
Elizabeth Schrimsher

Will came along just after the West had been fully settled and at a time when the nation was predominately agrarian. The railroad was bringing the era of the cattle drive to a close, and barbed wire was marking the end of open-range ranching. Factories were being built in the cities, while budding oil and mining industries fueled the appetite of a young nation. Agriculture was moving toward a market economy, using the railroads to ship food to the big population and manufacturing centers of the East. By the time of Will's death in 1935, the country had become an industrial giant with far-reaching economic and political influence in the world.

In this climate, Will Rogers came to personify what many people think of as a "pure American." He represented the twofold nature of our American psyche at that time. Although rooted in a rural and agricultural tradition, his life's journey took him to the heights of the media and technology of his day. While embracing the twentieth century, he held to the codes and values of a simpler time.

After the Civil War, the country was preoccupied with two things: securing the West and industrialization. These two endeavors ran hand in hand. Acquiring territory, expanding the railroads, developing natural resources, and systematizing agriculture were all needed to feed the industrial boom. The second half of the nineteenth century relentlessly transformed the West. While the industrialists expanded the areas of mining, transportation, and manufacturing, farmers and cattlemen pushed for the opening of more and more land to agriculture.

But the land was not free for the taking. The Indians, who had been living on the continent for over ten thousand years before Europeans arrived, fought bitterly to preserve their way of life in the face of overwhelming odds. Everything the Indians represented flew in the face of the settlers' most fundamental beliefs. They did not share the Europeans' religion or commitment to so-called progress.

They found themselves on a collision course with what white people called their "Manifest Destiny." The ramifications of such a collision between two fundamentally different cultures are extremely complex. But to put it simply, the Indians were lied to, coerced, outnumbered, and outgunned. It was only a matter of time before they would be completely overwhelmed.

As the Indians gradually succumbed to the advance, various nations had to be relocated. One of the more famous of these "great removals" was a forced march known as the "Trail of Tears." Through the winter months of September 1838 to February 1839, over fourteen thousand Cherokee men, women, and children were marched from Georgia, Tennessee, and the Carolinas to a reservation in what was to become Oklahoma. En route, over four thousand died from disease and exposure. They were buried in shallow graves alongside the trail. Will often referred to this travesty when speaking of the plight of the Indians under the rule of "the white man."

President Andrew Jackson, elected in 1828, rose to fame as an Indian fighter. He was notorious for his unrelenting pressure and cruelty toward the Indians. Of all the presidents, Jackson was the only one about whom Will had little nice to say.

In 1928, after attending a luncheon honoring the memory of Andrew Jackson, Will said this:

> *"Well, to tell you the truth, I am not so sweet on old Andy. He is the one that run us Cherokees out of Georgia and North Carolina. I ate the dinner on him, but I didn't enjoy it. I thought I was eating for Stonewall. Old Andy, every time he couldn't find any one to jump on, would come back and pounce onto us Indians. Course he licked*

the English down in New Orleans, but he didn't do it till the war had been over two weeks, so he really just fought them as an encore. Then he would go to Florida and shoot up the Seminoles. That was before there was a bathing suit in Palm Beach. Then he would have a row with the Government, and they would take his command and his liquor away from him, and he would come back and sick himself onto us Cherokees again. Then they sent the Indians to Oklahoma. They had a treaty that said, 'You shall have this land as long as grass grows and water flows.' It was not a good rhyme but looked like a good treaty, and it was...till they struck oil. Then the Government took it away from us again. They said the treaty only refers to 'Water and Grass; it don't say anything about oil.'

"So the Indians lost another bet. The first one was to Andrew Jackson, and the second was to Rockefeller, Doheny, Sinclair and Socony."[2]

Throughout Will's career, he was quite clear in his condemnation of how the Indians were treated. He criticized the cultural bias of his day, which he felt unfairly labeled Indians as "savages." Many of the tribes that the white people encountered while migrating west had sophisticated systems of law and government. Some had developed agriculture, while others followed the great herds of buffalo from Canada down into the Great Plains and lived a life as free as any people in history. Will doubted that our ways were as civilized as those the Indians had been practicing for centuries. The sarcasm just dripped off his statement, *"Something ought to be done about these 'Primitive' people who live off what nature provides. You would think they would get civilized, and learn to live off each other like us civilized folks do."*[3]

But those who were in sympathy with the plight of the Indian were few and far between. The fact that European Americans and Native Americans could never coexist as equals was well illustrated by the words of the famous general, William Tecumseh Sherman. In 1897, he said, "The more I see of these Indians, the more convinced I am that they all have to be killed or be maintained as a species of paupers." By the turn of the century, virtually all of the Indians had been forced onto reservations. Tens of thousands had either been killed through warfare or had died of diseases brought over from Europe.

The whites had a special designation for the Cherokees. They were called one of the "Five Civilized Tribes." After putting up a stiff fight in the East, the Cherokees realized that they would have to adapt to the inevitable presence of white people. They started accepting European customs, religion, and education. Many Cherokees intermarried with Europeans and became successful and prominent in their communities. This was the case with Will's parents, Clem and Mary.

Clem and Mary Rogers

Will's father had gotten in on the ground floor of the budding cattle industry. He was a very influential rancher, banker, judge, and political figure. He served on the commission that drew up the documents that were to make Oklahoma a state and was so highly respected in the community that Rogers County, Oklahoma, was named after him (not his son).

The raising of cattle was responsible for Will's early exposure to a special breed of worker – the cowboy. These men greatly influenced Will's values and humor. But there are two types of cowboys in our history: the real and the mythical. The real cowboys were rugged individuals who had a tough job. But unlike many Hollywood portrayals, they weren't all gunslingers, and many were not white. In Will Rogers' Indian Territory were Mexican vaqueros and black and Indian cowboys. In fact, the famous Chisolm Trail was established in 1867 by a half-Cherokee named Jesse Chisolm. Most often, white Europeans were the landowners and the bosses, but their employees came from many different races. The vast majority of young Will's playmates were the children of such people. His early interest in roping stemmed from the lessons he received as a child from Dan Walker, a freed slave who was Clem Rogers' top hand. Will was later drawn to fancy rope tricks and animal catches while on a trip to Chicago with his father in 1893. A wide-eyed thirteen-year-old boy got to see the great Mexican roper, Vincente Oropeza, performing in the Buffalo Bill Wild West Show at the Chicago World's Colombian Exposition that year. That experience planted one of the seeds to Will's future.

Although we still have cowboys today, the period depicted by Hollywood was short-lived. The cattle drives of movie fame lasted only from about 1867 to 1887. The arrival of the railroad and the breeding of heartier cattle in the colder climates closer to the railheads put an end to the twenty-year era of the big cattle drives. But fortunately, Will did get to drive some cattle in the Panhandle of Texas as a teenager. He was able to sleep out under the stars and listen to the humor and wisdom of his coworkers, many of whom were veterans of the glory days. The romance of this experience stayed with him for the rest of his life. He sometimes commented that he had been born too late for his true calling.

Things have come a long way since the old days. Feedlots and factory farming produce a lot of our cattle. But even so, the cowboy profession and many of its skills and traditions survive. Numerous ranches out west have preserved the old ways of working cattle, especially at roundup time. Even though many of today's ranchers drive pickup trucks and keep track of their business on personal computers, the West still has its share of roping, riding, rodeo, tall tales, and eccentric characters.

To get a handle on this, I once asked the most learned cowgirl I know to help me out. Sue Wallis knows cowboys. Every year she heads up the world's oldest and largest Cowboy Poetry Gathering in Elko, Nevada. I met her when I had the honor of performing my "Tribute" at that festive occasion in 1993. Looking out at an audience full of thousands of genuine cowboys and quite a few wanna-be's like myself, I figured I was in the right place to ask the question. "What exactly is a modern-day cowboy, anyway?" Sue told me that, in Nevada, not only are there cowboys, but there are also "buckaroos." I asked her what the difference was, and she said, "Well, cowboys don't line dance and buckaroos don't even watch."

Traveling around the West and mixing with its people has taught me a lot about the "Cowboy Way." This "way" involves both a code of behavior and a certain tendency to pack a lot of wisdom into a few words. A cowboy might say, "Lawyers help you get out of the kind of trouble you would have never gotten into if there weren't no lawyers," or "It's a darn sight easier to stand the smell of liquor than it is to listen to it." Will was exposed to this tradition early on, and it showed up in his quick little sayings like, *"I am no fisherman, and hope I never get lazy enough to take it up,"*[4] or *"It's not what you pay a man but what he costs you that counts,"*[5] or *"Everything is funny, as long as it is happening to somebody else."*[6]

Cowboys aren't above a little exaggeration, either. That's why the cowboy definition of an old-timer is "a feller who has had a lot of interesting experiences...and some of them are true." Perhaps this tendency toward overblowing the facts for the sake of the story is one of the reasons why a lot of mythology has grown up around the "Wild West." When we think back on those days, towns like Dodge City, Cheyenne, Tombstone, and Abilene come to mind. These towns' famous lawmen have had their exploits exaggerated so much over the years that they have become legends. But according to historian Kenneth C. Davis, there are more shooting incidents in a few months in any one of our larger modern cities than there ever were in the entire history of all these western towns combined. Today, we are far wilder in most respects than the "Wild West" ever was. Nevertheless, the cowboy has become a symbol of freedom and rugged individualism for people the world over. The myth of the cowboy fills novels, movies, television screens, and cigarette ads. This mythology isn't 100% true, to be sure, but it isn't a lie either. It's just half the story. We selectively amplify the moral messages we want to pass on to the next generation.

But the real West provides us inspiration without exaggeration. A closer look at the period when Will Rogers grew up reveals the great mettle it took to live in those days. The very real threats of weather, disease, infection, or injury—to say nothing of your neighbor—go far beyond anything a novelist or a screenwriter could invent. People had to draw upon their deepest personal resources to survive the rigors of daily life. Will Rogers, though possessed of a kind and gentle nature, was a product of just such a demanding environment. He came from a society of tough, mostly good-humored, self-reliant people. His father was quite successful, but Clem Rogers' success was achieved through hard work and self-sacrifice. Although Will was raised with everything he needed, he was expected to do hard physical labor just like everybody else.

If we were transported back to Will's early days, the first thing we'd have to do is lower our expectations. Not only was a modicum of comfort considered a blessing back then, but parents felt lucky if seven of their nine children lived to adulthood. Physical hardship, disease, and scarcity were just facts of life. The instant gratification we have come to expect through our technology and prosperity was nonexistent. Most people were relatively contented because they were largely unaware of the possibility that things could be much better. In our society, we seem to increase our expectation every time a new contribution to our comfort or convenience comes along; in Will's day, everything was new. The steady advance of technology was thrilling. The airplanes, automobiles, telephones, and movies that would be developed in Will's lifetime were not taken for granted. Books were filled with romantic stories about faraway places, while the idea of landing on the moon was still in the realm of science fiction. Advertising was in its infancy, so material envy was not as rampant as it is now. It was a society on which many of our older citizens reflect, saying, "We were poor, but we didn't know we were poor. Everybody we knew had the same things we did."

Will was not poor growing up. He had everything he needed except a mother. When Will was ten years old, Mary died of amoebic dysentery. Will was deeply grieved. A loving and attentive mother, she taught him to read before he ever went to school. Later in life, he spoke of her, saying, *"My mother's name was Mary, and if your mother's name is Mary and she was an old-fashioned woman, you don't have to say much for her. Everybody knows already."*[7]

Because he was at a loss as to how to deal with his growing son, Clem sent Will to various boarding schools. But Will didn't like school very much. He did well in things he enjoyed, like history, politics, and elocution, but he was too restless to apply himself to the subjects he didn't like. Playing the class clown, Will was constantly getting into trouble. He summed it all up by saying, *"After three years in McGuffey's Fourth Reader, I knew more about it than McGuffey did."*[8] Clem finally got so frustrated that he sent Will to Kemper Academy, a military school in Boonville, Missouri. But Will didn't care for that very much either. He said of the experience, *"I spent two years at Kemper. One was in the fourth grade and the other one was in the guardhouse...One was about as bad as the other."*[9]

Will was very bright, and a good argument could be made that the sterile school environment of his day was too stifling to maintain his interest. He had a formal education to what would be considered the tenth grade today. This was at a time when many people went only as far as the fourth grade, learned to read and write, and then went on to work at hard labor on a farm, a ranch, or in a factory. Even though Will quit Kemper after two years, his schooling demanded strong reading and memorization skills. As a result, he got a very good basic education. Will's career successes prove how much native intelligence he had, while his love of travel, technology, and current events give strong evidence of an inborn curiosity that flowered throughout his life.

After quitting Kemper, in 1898, Will went to Texas. At the Ewing Ranch, in the panhandle, he got a job as a $30-a-month cowboy. Soon after, he tried to join up with Teddy Roosevelt's Rough Riders. To his disappointment, they turned him away because he was too young. But adventure was beckoning, and it wouldn't be long before he would answer the call.

Betty Blake

Late in 1899, Will met his bride-to-be, Betty Blake. She was from Rogers, Arkansas. After a battle with typhoid fever,

Betty was recuperating in the company of her sister and brother-in-law who ran the train station at Oologah. Her first encounter with Will came when he tried to pick up a banjo he had ordered by mail. Terribly shy, he failed in his first attempt. He turned away, leaving the room without a word. On his second try, he successfully retrieved the package. Although Will was truly taken with Betty, he was a little intimidated. She was a lady and he was a bit country. But after a few false starts, he was able to establish a kind of awkward courtship. He then proceeded to set a pattern that would persist for the rest of their years together. Although he was love-struck, Will's love of travel pulled him away. He was not to see Betty for another two years.

Born too late to have done any open-range ranching, Will wanted to go to Argentina to see how it was done. In March of 1902, he set out with a friend, Dick Parris, on a trip to South America. Because of a lack of planning and poor connections, they went to Argentina by way of New Orleans, New York, England, Brazil, and Uruguay. Will worked with the gauchos for a while. Then, disillusioned by his inability to make a living in South America, he got a job on a steamship transporting livestock across the Atlantic Ocean. It was the worst job of his life. He got incredibly seasick, and in his letters home, he referred to his vessel as the "Floating Dung-Hill."

In late August, Will landed in South Africa, discouraged and homesick. He found work doing odd jobs at a ranch 150 miles inland from Durban and eventually landed another job that took him to Ladysmith. There he noticed an advertisement for a big event in town: Texas Jack's Wild West Show. He went into the main office looking for any kind of work that was available. But when he demonstrated his roping ability, Texas Jack hired him as a performer instead. He was billed as "THE CHEROKEE KID – Fancy Lasso Artist and Rough Rider." Later, Will joined the Wirth Brothers Circus, which took him to New Zealand and on to Australia. He ended up traveling around the world before he was twenty-five years old. His association with people of different races, religions, and customs gave him a worldly education that would serve him well later.

In 1904, Will returned home and joined the Colonel Mulhall Family Wild West Show out of Mulhall, Indian Territory. That show eventually took him to New York City and Madison Square Garden. At the Garden, a half ton of pot roast gave Will his first big break. A big steer jumped a barrier and climbed into the stands, sending panicked New Yorkers running for their lives. Will adeptly roped the critter and pulled him back into the arena. Flashbulbs were going off, and the next day the major headlines proclaimed Will Rogers a "hero." The resulting publicity gave him the name recognition he needed to break into the New York vaudeville scene. Continuing to build his career, Will slowly introduced a little commentary into his act. But at this point, he didn't have full confidence in his ability to talk on stage. He remained convinced that roping was his true strength. Betty Blake would help him change that perception of himself.

As Will's earning power became greater, he had more potential for stability. He continued to court Betty, often asking her to marry him. Finally, in 1908, she agreed. This marriage caused much consternation in Betty's home town. Will was part Indian, a world traveler, and in show business. Some of the folks in Rogers saw him as nothing more than a vagabond. All Will had to say about it was, *"The day I roped Betty I did the star performance of my life."*[10]

Throwing the 'Big Crinoline'– Keith's Union Square Theater

The newlyweds spent their early years together traveling on the vaudeville circuit. Before they were married, Will had promised Betty that he would eventually get out of show business. But each tour led to better offers – the "Big Time" was just around the corner. Both Will and Betty could see that given Will's nature and his improving prospects, keeping the promise would be impossible. Betty accepted the life and became her husband's biggest booster. It was she who encouraged him to put more commentary into his act. For Will to get up enough confidence to use his ropes as a support to the act, rather than the focus of it, took time. But dropping punch lines in coordination with butterflies, shoulder-rolls, and Texas skips paved the way to the more lucrative and prestigious venues in New York. By 1916, Will was a star attraction with the Ziegfeld Follies. His name became synonymous with the show. Accordingly, many of the Follies' wealthy patrons wanted Will to speak at their special dinners and banquets. Will's income and popularity were reaching new heights.

As the country became more industrial, tremendous fortunes were made as powerful men built huge financial empires. The political climate of the times was a conservative one. The government was committed to a laissez-faire approach to business, which left business leaders to make up their own rules, in most cases. The United States was starting to assert itself internationally, and the country was growing in power and influence.

The times were changing and so was Will Rogers. Known primarily for making comments from the stage, Will had yet to acquire the audience he would later command through his newspaper columns, radio programs, and talking movies. But his confidence was growing. He was becoming known for "calling 'em like he saw 'em." A prime example of this was in 1916, shortly before we entered World War I, when President Woodrow Wilson traveled some fifty miles from Washington, DC, to see a Friar's Club show that Will was doing in Baltimore. President Wilson had a thorn in his side in the form of a Mexican bandit, Pancho Villa. Villa had been making raids into the United States, and although the President had deployed General Pershing to catch him, the bandit continually eluded capture. Since one of Will's pet peeves throughout his career was what he saw as our country's lack of military preparedness, people sensed that Will might be lying in wait for the President. There was noticeable tension in the air as the audience waited to see whether Will would try to kid him about his policies. Although Will was nervous, not knowing how his jokes would be received, he leveled the following volley at Wilson:

> *"I see where they have captured Villa. Yes, they got him in the morning editions and then the afternoon ones let him get away.*

"Villa raided Columbus, New Mexico. We had a man on guard that night at the post. But to show you how crooked this Villa is, he sneaked up on the opposite side. We chased him over the line 5 miles, but run into a lot of government red tape and had to come back.

"There is some talk of getting a machine gun if we can borrow one. The one we have now they are using to train our army with in Plattsburg. If we go to war we will just about have to go to the trouble of getting another gun."[11]

Will later commented about the incident, saying: *"Now mind you, he* [Wilson] *was being rode on all sides for lack of preparations, yet he sat there and led that entire audience in laughing at the ones on himself."*[12]

Will never really attacked anyone. He claimed that the day he had to resort to a vicious style of humor would be the day that he quit the business. His belief was, *"If there is no malice in your heart there can be none in your gags."*[13] Will would just kid you a little, get you laughing and then tell you the truth. It may have been a little sneaky, but it was never mean-spirited. The President took it all in good humor, and Will's credibility moved up another notch.

When the United States finally did enter the "Great War," Will tried to join up. But he was rejected because of his advanced age and his large family. Both he and Betty were thirty-eight years old, and they had four children: Will Jr., Mary, Jim, and Freddie. Fortunately for Will's big family, his career was reaching new heights. He was recognized as a star nationwide. In 1917, Samuel Goldwyn (then Samuel Goldfish) was planning on making several films. One was *Laughing Bill Hyde*. The author of the story, Rex Beach, was a friend of both Will and Will's dear friend and fellow vaudevillian, Fred Stone. Rex wanted Will to play the lead role. At first, Will modestly refused, claiming he was no actor. But Rex and Fred finally talked him into it. The movie was filmed in New Jersey in 1918 and received very positive reviews. Will's movie career was under way. The next year, he moved his family to Hollywood where he went on to appear in some forty-nine more silent movies, for a total of fifty. Then the movies went from silent to talkies, and Will was in his element. He made twenty-one extremely successful talkies from 1929 to 1935, accumulating an impressive career total of seventy-one movies in all. But before leaving New York in 1919, Will increased his notoriety by launching his literary career. He released two collections of his Ziegfeld Follies commentaries: *The Cowboy Philosopher on the Peace Conference* and *The Cowboy Philosopher on Prohibition.* Will was breaking new ground, and his career was expanding by leaps and bounds.

But not all of the times were good times. In 1920, Will and Betty lost their two-year-old son, Freddie, in a diphtheria epidemic. Family tragedy was followed by financial difficulties later that year, when Will tried making movies with his own money. The most enduring of these was *The Ropin' Fool,* which preserved his roping artistry for all time. Apparently, Will could make good movies, but he was not very good at marketing them. He got into such deep financial trouble that, to maintain his lifestyle, he had to return to New York for the larger salaries offered by Mr. Ziegfeld.

Upon his return, Will was at no loss for action. New York was a Mecca for artists, writers, and performers of all kinds. It was the Roaring Twenties—a period marked by a wide-open approach to life, entertainment, and business. The scene was ripe for Will's next endeavor: a weekly newspaper column he started writing for the New York Times in 1922.

The following year, the McNaught Syndicate put it in over five hundred papers throughout the country. By 1926, it had evolved into the famous *Will Rogers Says*. At his peak, Will was being published daily and weekly, with a longer column on Sundays. Virtually everybody read Will's columns. Their popularity produced another book in 1924, *The Illiterate Digest*, which was a compilation of many of his most outstanding pieces. In 1922, he broadcast his first radio talk out of Pittsburgh. Radio was in its infancy, but Will was one of the first major stars to use it effectively.

Young Will on the radio

The wide-open business climate of the Twenties was supported by two very conservative presidents: Harding and Coolidge. Harding died in office, but his vice president, Calvin Coolidge, continued their laissez-faire approach to the business community. Coolidge was reelected in 1924. His economic philosophy was quite evident in his most famous quote, "The business of America is business." For his part, Will said of Coolidge, *"Calvin Coolidge is the first president to figure out that what the American people want is to be left alone."*[14] Coolidge's critics labeled him a "do-nothing" president, but Rogers joked, *"All of the prospective candidates study what to do, and who to do it to, and here comes Coolidge and does nothing and retires a hero, not only because he hadn't done anything but because he had done it better than anyone."*[15]

During Coolidge's administration Will traveled throughout the United States and Europe, by air whenever possible. In 1926, under contract with the *Saturday Evening Post,* he went to Europe and wrote numerous articles that were later compiled into his fourth book, *Letters of a Self-made Diplomat to His President.* That was followed, in 1927, by *There's Not a Bathing Suit in Russia and Other Bare Facts,* which chronicled Will's travels in the Soviet Union. The title stemmed from Will's having seen Russian men and women bathing publicly in the nude. Will said, *"While I did not get to see all of Russia, I got to see all of some Russians."*[16] In 1929, Will almost died from a gall bladder attack. Later that year, he wrote *Ether and Me or 'Just Relax,'* making fun of his brush with death and the surgeons who saved his life.

The decade of the Twenties brought many changes. Women had demanded and gotten the vote, communists were encouraging unrest among the working class, racism was on the rise with the reemergence of the Ku Klux Klan — and then there was Prohibition.

In 1919, the Temperance Movement, led mostly by women, got the eighteenth amendment to the Constitution passed, prohibiting the "manufacture, sale, or transportation of intoxicating liquors." The following year, the Volstead Act was passed to enforce the law. While some hold that Prohibition reduced the country's consumption of alcohol overall, those who wanted to drink were easily accommodated. In the 1920s, organized crime infiltrated many aspects of American life, as public officials were threatened, bribed, or otherwise coerced. America took on a new look as the period called "The Roaring Twenties" or "The Jazz Age" was launched. It spawned dance crazes, wild parties, bootlegged liquor, and a previously unheard-of freedom for women.

All of this was grist for Will Rogers' mill. Even though he was not much of a drinking man himself, Will opposed Prohibition. He thought it created more problems than it solved, and he criticized us for romanticizing its more violent and criminal elements. But Will must have been torn by this position. On the one hand, he saw prohibition as foolish, unenforceable, and corrupting. But on the other hand, as a comedian, he must have seen it as a blessing for the wealth of comic material its hypocrisy, corruption, and stretching of moral limits generated. Many of today's public figures provide us with the same service, and comedians always hate to see the more colorful ones fade away.

Calvin Coolidge made just such an exit in 1928, when he decided not to run for another term as president. Will hated to see him go. Not only was Coolidge's dour personality a perfect target for Will's jokes, but it happened that the two men were cordial acquaintances. On one occasion, Will imitated the president's voice on national radio. Later, Mrs. Coolidge told Will that she admired his impersonation but that she could do a much better imitation of her husband than Will could. Will responded with, *"I believe it, but look what you had to go through to learn it."*[17]

Instead of Coolidge, the Republicans ran an unsuspecting Herbert Hoover. With no idea that the country was moving toward financial disaster, Hoover accepted the nomination, and Calvin Coolidge made what turned out to be the wisest decision of his political career. As the Roaring Twenties roared, the country's economy was gradually rotting from within. It was a period of unprecedented financial speculation. Overextended credit, the buying of stocks on margin, and few controls on investors eventually dealt a death blow to an ailing economy that to all appearances looked robust and healthy. The stock market crashed in 1929, ushering in what was known as the Great Depression.

Will Rogers was fundamentally opposed to speculation. He had no investments himself, except in land. He was of an old school that frowned upon buying things on credit. Speculation was merely a legalized form of gambling in Will's book, used by those who wanted to avoid working. His pithy comments on the subject ran in this vein, *"If people could get that darn Wall Street off their minds. Half our people starving and the other half standing around a roulette wheel. They're going to get some easy money if they have to go broke to do it."*[18]

Will made jokes, but the reality of the country's financial ruin was quite grim. America had survived depressions before, but this was something different. As the economy continued to worsen, President Hoover held fast to the belief that the Depression was no more than a temporary setback. Elected at the height of prosperity, Hoover took much of the blame for the Great Depression by being unfortunate enough to be in office when everything collapsed. Beneath the surface, the ills of the economy had been developing for at least two administrations before Hoover came on the scene. But he and many others felt it was part of a normal business cycle that, given time, would right itself. This was a sincere belief that held the country's best interests at heart. Herbert Hoover's record as a private citizen, prior to his presidency, shows him to have been a great man and a model citizen. Will was acutely aware of this, and was kind to Mr. Hoover in all of his little jokes and commentaries. In 1931, Will said,

> *"Today is our President's fifty-seventh birthday. I look for him to come in for a lot of censure for allowing himself to get that old. If ever a man should be wished well, it should be him...Mr. Coolidge and Wall Street and big business had had their big party, and was just running out of liquor when they turned it over to Mr. Hoover. He arrived at the picnic when even the last hard-boiled egg had been consumed. Somebody slipped some Limburger cheese into his pocket and he got credit for breaking up the dance."* [19]

In 1932, Franklin Delano Roosevelt ran against Hoover and won. He offered the people what he called "A New Deal." Roosevelt's innovative but somewhat haphazard governing style was quite controversial. He would try something, and if it didn't work, he would drop it and try something else. Will kidded the new President by saying, *"They* [Big Business] *asked Mr. Roosevelt, 'Mr. Roosevelt, we never know what you're going to do next.' Roosevelt says, 'Neither do I!'"*[20] The new president's methods varied in their success and effectiveness. His programs and agencies provided jobs and built up the country's infrastructure, but many criticized them as wasteful make-work projects that concentrated too much power in Washington.

Will liked men who got things done. The country was in

crisis and Roosevelt was proposing solutions. After FDR had been in office for a few years, Will was more critical of his governing style. But early on, he expressed his support for the President this way,

> *"No money, no banks, no work, no nothing, but they know they got a man in there who is wise to Congress, wise to our big bankers and wise to our so-called big men. The whole country is with him. Even if what he does is wrong they are with him. Just so he does something. If he burned down the Capitol we would cheer and say, 'Well, we at least got a fire started anyhow.' We have had years of 'Don't rock the boat,' go on and sink it if you want to, we just as well be swimming as like we are."*[21]

Will donating a dime to John D. Rockefeller

As the Great Depression deepened, Will's career skyrocketed. He was personal friends with some of the most prominent figures in politics, industry, and show business. The nation's biggest power brokers listened closely as Will good-naturedly ribbed them for all their excesses and contradictions. Fortunately, for those hardest hit by the Depression, he always came at the "big boys" from the vantage point of the average citizen. Without Will Rogers, the rich and powerful might never have heard a word about what the "regular bird" was going through.

In calling attention to the plight of the suffering masses, Will was not one to sit idly by and wait for someone else to solve the problems generated by unemployment, poverty, and bad weather. All through the early 1930s, he kept up a backbreaking schedule of benefit performances to help the less fortunate. He did relief work for people hit by the ravages of nature. He did benefits that kept theaters open and saved jobs in his own profession. He even went to Nicaragua to witness the aftermath of a devastating earthquake. The scene so moved him that he came home and generated millions in aid for the suffering Nicaraguans. To express their gratitude, in 1939, the Nicaraguan government issued five commemorative stamps in his honor.

Will's charitable work is far too extensive to cover here. But to give you a sense of his generosity, I will share a tale told to me by Will's grandniece, Doris "Coke" Meyer, my host for a performance at the Civic Center in Bartlesville, Oklahoma, in January 1995. As Coke drove me around town, showing me all of the wonders that Mr. Phillips' oil company had brought to Bartlesville, she told of how her Great Aunt Betty, after Will's death, would often come to visit Oklahoma. Betty told a story about how she used to send Will off to the studio in the morning with what she thought would be enough money to get him through the day. But Will would always come home with nothing left in his pockets. Betty kept increasing the amounts, from $50 to $75 to $100 and so on. But Will would always come home broke. Finally, she asked where the money was going. Coke paraphrased Will's answer with something like, "Well, Blake. Old Jim got pushed into part-time work last week so he was a little short. And John lost his job completely so I gave him some. We all wanted to go out for lunch but half the boys couldn't afford it so I picked up that. I heard that Dave's son needed an operation so I saw that he got a little help to get that boy in shape. Then on the way home I saw an old down-and-outer on the street and he looked like he had been rode and broke…so I gave the rest to him." At the time Coke told me this story, I was reading some Oriental philosophy and ran across the phrase, "A fool loses all of his money…but a Great Fool gives all of his money away." If Will Rogers was any kind of a fool, I would say he was a great one!

It comes as no surprise that when Will Rogers and Wiley Post died in a plane crash near Point Barrow, Alaska, on August 15, 1935, the nation was stunned. People felt as if they had lost family members when these two men passed on. Many wondered what it would be like to continue the struggle with hard times without the reassuring words and good humor of Will Rogers.

Although Will wasn't reckless, he wasn't overly careful either. No doubt his philosophical lack of a fear of death contributed to putting him in harm's way. In those days, exploratory aviation was a risky business. But Will was a doer and he greatly enjoyed pushing his limits. One might wonder, had Will a choice in the matter, whether he would have chosen dying in a plane crash over the gradual deterioration that often accompanies old age. At the time, Will was at his peak, full of life. He had circumnavigated the globe three times, and there he was, off on another adventure. He was living a life fuller than many of us could ever imagine. Even so, that was little comfort to those left behind. The expressions of loss offered by everyone from heads of state to the "regular birds" indicated how sorely Will Rogers would be missed.

Will Rogers and Wiley Post

But as for Will, he simply said, *"When I die, my epitaph, or whatever you call those signs on gravestones, is going to read, 'I joked about every prominent man of my time, but I never met a man I didn't like.' I am so proud of that. I can hardly wait to die so it can be carved. And when you come to my grave, you'll probably find me sittin' there proudly reading it."*[22]

2

BACON AND BEANS BUT NO EXTREMES

Will Rogers came from a period in our history that was marked by self-sufficiency. His people were tough and hard-working. But in the early 1930s, work was hard to find. The material dreams of our relatively young nation were caught in the grip of the Great Depression. We hung our hopes on the promises of science and technology while experimenting with the progressive thinking and innovative approaches of Franklin Delano Roosevelt's "New Deal." Will's opinions were influenced both by his self-sufficient upbringing and by the new ideas of his day. This made for an interesting mix that was politically neither right nor left.

In many ways, Will was a Populist. He believed in capitalism, but he didn't think the little people should get run over in the process. He sided with the farmer and the worker but understood the dynamics of the marketplace as well. The Populist Movement of the 1890s was rooted in rural America, where farmers and their neighbors held the conviction that rich and powerful interests were dispossessing the common people of their participation in the economic and political process. Far from radical, these people were the salt of the earth, trying to better their situation. This is why today, whenever politicians want to claim they are returning "power to the people," they call themselves "Populists."

Because of Will's upbringing, he had a natural affinity with rural and working people. Although he never officially aligned himself with any political party, he let his populist sympathies show in 1931. The Depression was deepening, and the combination of bad weather, a crashed market, and a ruined economy were being felt by the farmer.

COMBINE SPEECH

"You town waddies know what a Combine is?

"Well here is all it does...just one machine and in one trip over the ground. On the front end of it is an arrangement that makes a deal to take over the ground from the bank that is holding the present mortgage. Then right behind that gadget on this big machine is a thing that grubs up the Roots and Herbs. Another thing right behind that grinds up the Roots and Herbs into 'Sagwa' Indian Medicine, which is sold by a White man who says he was adopted into the Indian tribe. Then just a few feet behind that, all connected with the same machine, are the plows that plow the ground. Then right in the furrow is the seeder, then another plow that plows the furrow back where it was in the first place. Then comes the fertilizer, and then the sickle that cuts the grain. Then it's carried along a little platform into the Threshing Machine where it's threshed, then out and into sacks, and into the big Grain Elevator that is fastened onto the thing.

"Then on near the back end is a stock market board where a bunch of men that don't own the farm, the wheat, or the Combine, buy it back and forth from each other. That is if you have threshed a thousand Bushels why they sell each other a million bushels of this thousand bushels which was actually threshed. Then they announce to the farmer that on account of supply and

demand, the wheat is only worth two bits. That's what you call a Combine."[1]

In many ways, Will's political beliefs defy categorization. "Highly independent with a strong dose of skepticism" might fit. By trade and inclination, Will was primarily a reporter. He was interested in the facts and distrusted ideologues. He had what one might call a "Big Carrot/Big Stick" philosophy. If people wanted to work or educate themselves to improve their lots in life, Will thought they should have the chance. Society should invest in its people, hold out incentives for them to succeed, and justly reward them for their contributions. This was the Big Carrot. On the other hand, Will had little patience with laziness. He issued strong indictments against those who would bend the rules or cause harm to others. He felt that the full weight of the law should be brought to bear on wrongdoers. This was the Big Stick.

Regardless of circumstances, Will's take on the human condition was always tempered by a fair and compassionate nature. This was best illustrated in one of his most famous speeches, a radio broadcast made on October 18, 1931. He was invited to share the air waves with President Herbert Hoover, who had asked him to lend his support to the President's Organization on Unemployment Relief. As the reality of the Great Depression sank into the minds of the general public, Mr. Hoover had become so unpopular that the squatters' camps full of the unemployed and their families were being called "Hoovervilles," and the gesture of pulling out your empty pockets was called "showing your Hoover money." The President felt that Will had the ear of the people and could provide a note of levity to the proceedings. He was right about the first point but only partially right about the second. Although Will's speech was gentle and humane, it was more serious than expected. There were a few gentle jests, but his contribution overall was an elegant off-the-cuff indictment of the excesses of the 1920s. Will called for understanding and aid to the suffering millions, and this became known as his famous

BACON, BEANS, AND LIMOUSINES SPEECH

"Now don't get scared and start turning off your radios. I'm not advertising or trying to sell you anything. If the mouthwash you are using is not the right kind and it tastes sort of like sheep-dip, why you'll just have to go right on using it. I can't advise any other kind at all. And if the cigarettes that you are using, why if they don't lower your Adam's apple, why I don't know of any that will. You will just have to cut out apples, I guess. That's the only thing I know.

"Now, Mr. Owen Young asked me to annoy on this program this evening. You all know Mr. Owen D. Young. You know, he's the only sole surviving wealthy Democrat, so naturally when a wealthy Democrat asks me to do anything I have to do it, see?

"Well, Mr. Young, he's head of the Young Plan, you know. He's the originator of the Young Financial European Plan. He's head of the Young Men's Temperance Union, and originator of Young's Markets, and Young Kippur. And was the first Democratic child born of white parents in Youngstown, Ohio.

"He started the Young Plan in Europe. That was that every nation pay just according to what they could afford to pay, see? And, well, somebody else come along with an older plan than Young's plan, and it was that nobody don't pay anybody anything, and course that's the oldest

plan there is. And that's the one they are working under now. That's why we ain't getting anything from Europe.

"So when Mr. Young asked me to appear, why I said, 'Well, I'm kind of particular. Who is going to be the other speaker? Who else is on the bill with me?'

"And he said, 'Well, how would Mr. Hoover do?'

"Well, I slightly heard of him, you know, and I said, 'Well, I'll think it over.' So I looked into Mr. Hoover's record and inquired of everybody, and after I had kind of thrown out about two-thirds of what the Democrats said about him, why I figured that I wouldn't have much to lose by appearing with Mr. Hoover, so I'm here this evening appearing on the bill with Mr. Hoover. So now I expect you won't hear any more of 'Amos and Andy'; it will just be Hoover and Rogers from now on.

"Now we read in the papers every day, and they get us all excited over one or a dozen different problems that's supposed to be before this country. There's not really but one problem before the whole country at this time. It's not the balancing of Mr. Mellon's budget. That's his worry. That ain't ours. And it's not the League of Nations that we read so much about. It's not the silver question. The only problem that confronts this country today is at least 7,000,000 people are out of work. That's our only problem. There is no other one before us at all. It's to see that every man that wants to is able to work, is allowed to find a place to go to work, and also to arrange some way of getting more equal distribution of the wealth in the country.

"Now it's Prohibition, we hear a lot about that. Well, that's nothing to compare to your neighbor's children that are hungry. It's food, it ain't drink that we are worried about today. Here a few years ago we were so afraid that

the poor people was liable to take a drink that now we've fixed it so that they can't even get something to eat.

"So here we are in a country with more wheat and more corn and more money in the bank, more cotton, more everything in the world...there's not a product that you can name that we haven't got more of than any other country ever had on the face of the earth...and yet we've got people starving. We'll hold the distinction of being the only nation in the history of the world that ever went to the poor house in an automobile. The potter's fields are lined with granaries full of grain. Now if there ain't something cockeyed in an arrangement like that, then this microphone here in front of me is...well, it's a cuspidor, that's all.

"Now I think that perhaps they will arrange it...I think some of our big men will perhaps get some way of fixing a different distribution of things. If they don't they are certainly not big men and won't be with us long, that's one thing.

"These people that you are asked to aid, why they are not asking for charity, they are naturally asking for a job. But if you can't give them a job, why the next best thing you can do is see that they have food and the necessities of life. You know, there's not a one of us has anything that these people that are without it now haven't contributed to what we've got. The most unemployed or the hungriest man in America has contributed in some way to the wealth of every millionaire in America. It wasn't the working class that brought this condition on at all. It was the big boys themselves who thought that this financial drunk we were going through was going to last forever. They over...merged and over...capitalized, and over...everything else. That's the fix that we're in now.

Will Rogers on the radio

"Now, I think that every town and every city will raise this money. In fact, they can't afford not to. They've got the money because there's as much money in the country as there ever was. Only fewer people have it, but it's there. And I think the towns will all raise it because I've been on a good many charity affairs all over the country and I have yet to see a town or a city ever fail to raise the money when they knew the need was there, and they saw the necessity. Every one of them will come through.

"Europe don't like us and they think we're arrogant,

*and bad manners, and have a million faults, but every one of them, well, they give us credit for being liberal.**

"Doggone it, people are liberal. Americans, I don't know about America being fundamentally sound and all that after-dinner hooey, but I do know that America is fundamentally liberal. Now, I want to thank Mr. Gifford, the head of this unemployment, thank Mr. Young, and I certainly want to thank Mr. Hoover for the privilege of being allowed to appear on the same program with him. Because I know that this subject is very dear to Mr. Hoover's heart and know that he would rather see the problem of unemployment solved than he would to see all the other problems he has before him combined. And if every town and every city will get out and raise their quota, what they need for this winter, why it will make him a very happy man, and happiness hasn't been a steady diet with our president. He's had a very tough, uphill fight, and this will make him feel very good. He's a very human man. I thank you. Good night."[3]

Notice the tone of this speech. Will was not attacking his host. There was no anger or resentment in his delivery. He was very understanding of Mr. Hoover's difficult position. Will was firm, but at the same time, he appealed to his audience's better nature and sense of decency. He always took the high road and, although Will disagreed with many presidents, he never failed to treat their office with complete respect.

Now just because Will was for helping people who were down on their luck didn't mean he thought government relief was the answer to all of the country's problems. In "Bacon, Beans, and Limousines" he was calling for aid from private sources. Later, when a lot of government programs were being introduced, Will started to feel what many of us are feeling today. He said, "*You know, there is dozens of great humanitarian things that could be done at very little cost, if the tax was properly applied. It's the waste in government that gets everybody's goat.*[4] *The crime of taxation is not in the taking it, it's in the way that it's spent.*"[5]

In talking with Jim Rogers, Will's youngest son, I found that there was another reason Will was hard to categorize politically. Jim told me that his father had his convictions, but that he was first and foremost a comedian. This is how Will expressed the need for neutrality while performing on stage: "*We are paid by an audience to entertain them, not to instruct them politically. While the things you say may please one part of your audience it may displease the other part, and as one pays just as much to get in as another, we want to be friendly with each. So distribute your compliments and your knocks so when the audience goes out they don't know where you are politically.*"[6]

At the same time, Will held earnestly to his independent status and his right to speak his mind, saying, "*I think I am as independent as anyone writing. I have as many Republican as Democratic papers, as many readers that can't read as can. The editorial policies of these great dailies mean nothing to me, I am going to call 'em like I see 'em.*"[7]

Will couldn't resist the urge to skewer people if he felt it was needed. Their party affiliations were of little consequence to him. He hung onto the middle ground from where he could deflate what he saw as extreme viewpoints on either side. Fascists and dictators felt his barbs, and he was very hard on socialists and communists. The Russians had been engaged in a bloody revolution. The new Bolshevik regime was consolidating its power while brutalizing its own people. Communist zealots were preaching world domination and, by 1919, a "Red Scare" had gripped the nation. The public perceived communists as bomb throwers, bent on bringing the country down.

COMMUNISM AND SOCIALISM

"You know if there is one thing a Communist can do it is explain. You can ask him any question in the world, and if you give him long enough he will explain their angle, and it will sound plausible then. Communism to me is one-third practice and two-thirds explanation.[8]

"I have come to the conclusion that the reason there is so many books on Socialism is because it's the only thing in the world that you can't explain easy. It's absolutely impossible for any Socialist to say anything in a few words. You say, 'Is it light or dark?' and it takes him two volumes to answer Yes or No; and then you know there is a catch in it somewhere. More words ain't good for anything in the world only to bring on more argument. If the Socialists worked as much as they talked, they would be the most prosperous style of Government in the World.

"This guy Marx, why, he was like one of these efficiency experts. He could explain to you how you could save a million dollars and he couldn't save enough himself to eat on...He never did a tap of work only write propaganda...He wrote for the dissatisfied, and the dissatisfied is the fellow who don't want to do any manual labor. He always wants to figure out where he and his friends can get something for nothing.

"Most of these fellows were on little Communist Newspapers. Now America has withstood some pretty rough handling at times, but I sure would hate to see it fall under the management of a troop of our

Dissatisfied Newspaper men.

"You know a Communist's whole life work is based on complaint of how everything is being done. Well, when they are running everything themselves, why, that takes away their chief industry. They have nobody to blame it on. Even if he is satisfied with it, why, he is miserable because he has nothing to complain about. Same way with strikes and Revolutions. They would rather stir up a strike than eat. So, naturally, in Russia with themselves, they feel rather restrained, for they are totally unable to indulge in their old favorite sport of going on strike and jumping on a box and inviting all the boys out with them. You make one satisfied and he is no longer a Communist. So if they ever get their country running good they will defeat their own cause.

"But you know, you can't condemn everybody just because they started a Revolution. We grabbed what little batch of liberty we used to have through a revolution. But I don't think anyone, like Mr. Lenin, that just made a business of proposing them for a steady diet, would be the one to pray to and try and live like. We all know a lot of things that would be good for our Country, but we wouldn't want to go so far as propose that everybody start shooting each other till we got them. A fellow shouldn't have to kill anybody just to prove they are right.

"Now, mind you, I may be wrong about these people, for you can never tell about a Russian. They all may be just having the best time in the World over there and enjoying it all fine. You know, that is one thing about the Russian, he thrives on adversity. He is never as happy in his life as when he is miserable. So he may just be setting pretty, for he is certainly miserable. It may be just the

land for a Comrade to want to hibernate in.

"But I tell ya, there was some days when I was over there, it would really look to me like they were trying to do something, and were going to get somewhere; and the next day you would see stuff that would make you think, 'What has all these millions of innocent, peaceloving people done that through no fault of their own they should be thrown into a mess like this, with no immediate prospects of relief?' So I am going to be honest with you – I don't know whether to kiss 'em or kill 'em."[9]

3

COMMIT THE CRIME, DO THE TIME

Today one of our most important issues is crime. Public opinion polls show that people fear for their personal safety and the security of their homes more than they fear for their jobs or their health. They resent the negative example criminal behavior sets for their children. The same was true in Will's day. Here's what he had to say about one of the "heroes" of his day: *"Why just two weeks ago I had a two hour interview with Al Capone. But there was absolutely no way I could write it and not make a hero out of him. Everybody you talk to would rather hear about Capone than anybody you ever met. What's the matter with an age when our biggest gangster is our greatest national interest?"*[1]

During Prohibition, crime rates soared. Many felt that law enforcement was ineffective and that the legal system was a farce. Will's comments in those days reflected the public's concerns. See if these lines don't sound like the complaints you hear today.

CRIME

"Oh we are living in progress. All of our boasted inventions, like the Auto and the Automatic, and our increased 'Dope' output, terrible liquor, lost confidence in our Justice, Graft from top to bottom, all these have made

it possible to commit anything you can think of and in about 80 percent of the cases get away with it. I tell ya, give any young Egotist two shots of dope and an Automatic these days and he will hold up the Government Mint.[2]

Will Rogers from *Lightnin'*

"Why just last week they had a robbery in Los Angeles. And due to the bravery of a bank official and the efficiency of the police, two robbers were killed. They caught all the rest. I think it was four captured. Well, I wish you could read the crime and jail records of all those six men. They had been pardoned or paroled from every institution in the State at least once a month for the last fifteen years. Their records read like they had just played a series of one-night stands in each jail. They wasn't prisoners. They were traveling men, making hotels out of jails, and that's not an unusual case in any State.[3]

"It must be awfully monotonous belonging to one of

these State pardon boards. There is days and days when they just have to sit around waiting for new criminals to be caught so they can pardon 'em.[4]

"But it does simplify things. All you have to do to find out who the criminal is nowadays is just find the one that's been pardoned the most times.[5] *When have you read anywhere of a crime being committed by an amateur?"*[6]

Looking at television, we tend to think that the media's tabloid mentality is something that came along recently. Not so. The public has always had an appetite for sensationalism. Make no mistake, we were just as fascinated with crime, sex, and violence in Will's day as we are today. The difference is that we've now had a steady diet of it for the last 60 years, and tabloid television has upped the ante to the point that our children are being exposed to footage of actual crimes, violence, and sometimes death. No wonder we find ourselves becoming, if not angry, at least a little jaded by it all. Well, there is nothing like a little sarcasm to cheer you up when you're feeling cynical. Here's a sarcastic Will driving home his point.

CRIME AND THE MEDIA

"You know, Chicago has been receiving tremendous amounts of advertising on their crime waves, while Detroit was having just as many casualties and not getting one tenth the publicity out of it. They were becoming down right discouraged. But you see, here was a town that had been so anxious to advertise the amount of motor cars that was made there, that we never thought of it as any thing else than a mere grist mill, grinding out things for installments. But I told 'em that they gotta quit yapping about their production and start talking about their destruction.

One car being destroyed is 20 times of more interest to readers than a thousand cars being made. Deaths get twice the notice that births do in papers. Nobody wants to know who was born, but everybody is anxious to know who dies, and the better known they are, the more anxious they are to read about their death.

"How many cars you made, and how much your population increased, comes under the heading of nothing but statistics...and nobody is interested in numbers. They are dull reading. Pick out one of your good murders that you are going to have and concentrate on it. Don't lump 'em all together in the news every day. Don't pick too complicated a one or the people won't be able to understand it. Get some Church member mixed up in it if possible, and you wont have much trouble along that line. Have a pretty good dash of scandal. Make your scandal look like human interest. Get the tabloids on it. Now, you can take a murder like that and build it up properly and make it look like something.

"Course, Machine Guns have helped Chicago. The novelty of the weapon has as much to do with it as the prominence of the ones annihilated. Detroit is still shooting with pistols. Get some Airoplanes going, and drop some bombs from the air by one Gang onto another. Then you will have it on Chicago. This is a day, and time of progress, and new things. All this is what I told the Mayor of Detroit, and you just notice, from now on, if you don't see an improvement in publicity with Detroit's crime."[7]

Often Will seemed to see a little foreshadowing of the future. Even though he was in the middle of Prohibition, he saw where the big money was eventually going to wind up – not in liquor, but in drugs. In those days, the average person had little knowledge of this problem. Now, most of our incarcerated criminals have been sentenced for drug-related crimes.

DRUGS

"Let me tell you about one Mr. Richard Pearson Hobson. He was our outstanding Hero of the Spanish American war. Well, he is connected with a wonderful work. He is now the head of the Anti-narcotic work in this country. Say, let him tell you what is happening to the youth of this country through drugs. Talk about our crime waves, it's nothing but 'Heroin,'...that's all the crime wave is. They have got to rob to supply the dope. Talk about profit in things. Opium from the time a certain amount leaves its original owner in China, until it is split up into all its various ingredients and passes through all the hundreds of hands, increases in value nine thousand times. That is, a grain of it sells eventually for nine thousand times as much as it originally cost. Talk about bootlegging and doubling your money; the dope dealer is the Ford of the bootleggers."[8]

Seems like every time we turn around, some federal agency has somebody surrounded. These standoffs make big news. It's pretty amazing how many people it takes to arrest somebody. Will had a funny take on this phenomenon:

"So how do we go about catchin' these big time crooks anyhow? Well, the government is arranging a war chest of three million to hire and equip more men in the crime drive; 200 speedy armored cars, submachine guns, bullet-proof vests and tear gas. But it seems to me that two hundred armored cars can't very secretly drive up to

your place of hiding without being detected in advance.

"You know, in the days when they caught these fellows, it was by one Pinkerton detective following them, or one Texas Ranger, or one Northwest Mounted Police. I bet we got a lot of good man hunters in our various forces, if they were allowed to work without carrying an orchestra with 'em."[9]

And finally, when it comes to a media circus, you can't beat the high-profile trial, especially if the defendant is famous. Even in Will's day, the public sentiment was that the legal system was highly ineffective.

JUSTICE

"What happens if we do get lucky and happen to catch one of these robbers, dope dealers or murderers? Well, take this murderer they have out there in California. His name is Hickman. He confessed, so that means a long-drawn-out trial. It's going to be a fight to a finish between the alienists [psychiatrists] *and the photographers.*

"American murder procedure is about as follows: Foul enough to commit a crime, dumb enough to get caught, smart enough to prove you was crazy when you committed it and fortunate enough to show you was too sane to hang.[10]

"Compare that to British style justice. There was a famous case being tried in England where a fellow had swindled the people out of ten million dollars through fake stock transactions. They just gave him fourteen years so fast that it took all the Americans' breath away and all they talked about after that was English justice compared to ours. It was the consensus of opinion, that if it had been in the U.S., he would have gone into vaudeville

or the Senate. None of the habus corpusing and suspended sentences or appealing it when you commit a crime over there. You just wake up surrounded by a small space.[11]

"But over here we're more civilized. Trials have to go on a long time over here. Well, all I know is that it should not take a nation or a State seven years to decide whether anyone committed a crime or not. It's a good thing these criminals are young men when their crime is committed, otherwise they wouldn't live long enough for justice to make up its mind.[12]

"Of all the cockeyed things we got in this country at the present time, it's some of our judges, and courts, and justices. They gotta do something with the crooks while they're making up their minds. So what's the result? We got more bandits out on bond than we got people for 'em to rob, that's what.[13]

"If we ever do get them into prison, I have a new plan for our prison system. Of course this may be a radical suggestion, but couldn't they fix some way where the guards carried the guns instead of the prisoners?[14]

"Well, I don't know what to do about all this. It's just that these days we don't seem to be able to even check crime. So if we can't even check it, why not legalize it? Yea!...put a heavy tax on it. We have taxed other industries out of business; it might work here."[15]

Now we come to one of those subjects that generates a lot of heat these days. On May 27, 1993, I had the honor of performing for the Oklahoma State Society at the National Press Club in Washington, DC. Before the performance, a festive chili dinner was served (chili was Will Rogers' favorite dish). While I was mingling with the guests, my host,

Lou Priebe, approached me, saying that Washington's most dedicated Will Rogers fan was waiting to meet me in the next room. When I entered the room, there, sitting in his wheelchair, was Jim Brady, prominent Republican and former press secretary to President Ronald Reagan. In 1981, Jim suffered a head injury from a stray bullet when a madman tried to assassinate President Reagan. Since that time, Jim and his wife, Sarah, have been major advocates for gun control. They promoted and got passed into law the Brady Bill, which mandates a customer waiting period and background check before a handgun can be purchased.

Jim Brady and Lance Brown

Jim and I discussed our favorite subject, Mr. Rogers, for about twenty minutes. Then, as we headed into the auditorium for the performance, Jim mentioned that it was a shame how few heroes of Will's caliber we have with us today. Lou said, "I don't know about you, Lance, but when I think of heroes, I think of Jim Brady." I remember Jim saying, "Don't be silly. I wouldn't be qualified to shine Will Rogers' boots."

Probably many gun supporters will heartily disagree with the following speech. Even so, I must stay true to Will's viewpoint. Many times people are careless in quoting Will Rogers. They paraphrase him inaccurately or take him out of context. Some ignore the bulk of what he had to say on a particular subject in order to make it look as if Will shared their political bias. By accidentally or intentionally leaving out a few key words, one can easily distort Will's true meaning. Whether innocent or deliberate, such errors do an injustice to Will Rogers and to history.

GUNS

"Well, all I know is just what fills up the papers, and naturally that ain't much. The biggest question that is agitating the Public is the following: 'Are all escaped Lunatics to be furnished with guns and ammunition?' This gun thing is getting pretty serious here around New York. Everybody that hasn't got a gun is being shot by somebody. A Flask and a Gun are now considered standard equipment, and are supposed to accompany every tough kid when he steps into long pants. They could start searching everybody and in one day here they would get enough Pistols and Stilettos to dam up the Hudson River.

"I was born and raised in the Indian Territory, at Claremore to be exact. (A town that has cured more people than Florida has swindled). Well, that country, along about the time I was a yearling, was supposed to have some pretty tough men. Of course, as I grew up and we began to be able to uphold law and righteousness, these men gradually began to thin out and drift on down into Politics, a big part of them becoming Governors. Well, even in those days out there it was against the law to carry guns and every once in awhile the Sheriff would

search a fellow to see if he was overdressed…and they fined 'em heavy. Mind you, that was men carrying guns that knew what they were; knew the danger of them, and knew how to use them.

"A bad man in those days consisted of a careful, deliberate, cool-headed, steel-nerved individual who was really a protector of women and children, or innocent people. But here nowadays, the so-called bad man is either an escaped Lunatic or a thick-headed Hop fiend or somebody full of terrible liquor. He shoots people just to get his picture in the paper. Some of our Newspapers, if you take the murders out of them, would have nothing left but the title of the paper. To compare one of the numbskull killers now-a-days with a Jesse James or a Bob Dalton would almost be sacrilegious. Still these addle brains can go and buy a gun any place they want to.

"You know what has been the cause of the big increase in murders? It's been the manufacture of the automatic pistol. It's all right to have it invented, but it should never have been allowed outside the Army, and then only in war times. The Automatic pistol is as much more dangerous and destructive than the old six-shooter, as poison gas is over perfume. In the first place there is no skill or nerve required in using it. You just touch a trigger and aim the thing around like you would a sprinkling can or a hose. It is shooting all the time, and the more unsteady the nerve of the holder, why, the better the shooting he can do, because he takes in a bigger radius.

"When a man used to have to know something about a gun, and have the nerve to take aim at the party being used as a target, there was at least some skill and dignity connected with the profession. But if these City Killers had to learn how to shoot before shooting somebody, we

absolutely know there wouldn't be as much killing, because you can look at them and tell they would never have had sense and patience enough to have learned to shoot. You let the Government confiscate and forbid the entire sale of automatics, even to officers, (because officers kill 10 innocent people to 1 guilty one with those sprinkling cans) and prohibit guns of even the older variety to any but officers, and when you catch a Guy with one send him to Jail...not fine him.

"But I see where a lot of men are advocating letting everybody carry guns with the idea that they will be able to protect themselves. In other words, just make a Civil War out of this Crime Wave. When you see a man coming and he looks like he hasn't got as much as you and might want to rob you, why, just open up on him with your miniature Gatling gun. Now, he may start shooting at you thinking you are trying to murder him or rob him. So let every man protect himself. 'No policeman necessary.' That is the slogan of these people.

"If you think that being armed protects you, why, how about the amount of Policemen that are shot down here in New York? They are all armed. Yet these Hop Heads shoot 'em and all with automatics, because they wouldn't have the nerve to do it with anything else. Of course, the surest way out of the whole thing would be to punish them. But, of course, that is out of the question...that's barbarous, and takes us back, as the hysterics say, to the days before Civilization.

"So if it's a small crime, we fine them; and if it's confessed murder, why, it's Insanity. Alienists are busier and get more than Policemen. We go on the theory that if you confess you must be insane. In the old days a man would go to any extremes to keep from getting into a shooting

affray when he was under the influence of liquor, because he knew he was at a disadvantage. But now, the more drunk or drugged he is, the more people he will hit. So if you are going to do away with Capital punishment and sell guns to everybody, let's fix it so the party behind the gun will be at least a clear-headed, skilled marksman instead of a drunken amateur. Think of the humiliation of being shot by one of our present-day Bandits!"[16]

4

WILL'S COUNTRY—RIGHT AND WRONG

In the period following World War I, most Americans just wanted to get back to normal. There was a strong isolationist tendency running through the nation. And although Will was not in complete agreement with the more selfish motivations behind this isolationism, he was a major advocate of the United States' minding its own business. He did not believe in the military adventurism that had been prevalent in the years just before the war. Will felt our two best friends were the Atlantic and the Pacific Oceans and that we should be militarily prepared but keep the troops at home. The war in Europe was settled through an armistice. It had created much suffering, with no clear victory for either side. According to Will, the whole thing was a terrible waste of time, money, and human life. But mostly he saw it as someone else's fight.

That did not mean that Will turned his back on human suffering. When people were in need, whether in a neighboring town or a neighboring country, Will was always there to help out. This was in sharp contrast to the attitude of most of the isolationists of his day. Many of them would advocate not getting involved when people were starving but would suddenly become international bullies if they felt it was to their advantage. Will once wrote,

"Up to now our calling card to Mexico or Central

> *America had been a gunboat or a bunch of Violets shaped like Marines. We could never understand why Mexico wasn't just crazy about us; for we had always had their good-will, and Oil and coffee and minerals, at heart.*[1] *Ya know, when one nation is big and one is little, why the little nation's port is just like a public regatta. Everybody can come in that's got a boat. The whole thing as I see it all over the world today is that the little nations have got no business being little.*[2] *I don't care how little your country is, you got a right to run it like you want to. When the big nations quit meddling then the world will have peace.*[3] *Take the sugar out of Cuba and we would no more be interested in their troubles than we would a revolution among the Zulus."*[4]

Much has changed since Will made these statements. In early August of 1945, World War II culminated in the atomic bombing of Hiroshima and Nagasaki. The Japanese formally surrendered on August 14, thus making August 15, 1945, the first full day of peace in the Nuclear Age. This was exactly ten years after Will Rogers and Wiley Post perished in a plane crash in Alaska. What would Will's opinions on warfare and minding our own business have been had he lived through those ten years? Would the Cold War, with its Berlin Wall, and the Korean War, with its demilitarized zone, have found Will still insisting that our military might "only be used on the home grounds"? With nuclear annihilation as part of the equation, would the Cuban Missile Crisis have changed Will's mind regarding our role in world affairs? Where would he have come down on the Viet Nam War? on how it was run? on the way it divided the country? What would he think of the ultimate irony that our bitterest enemies of over fifty years ago are now among our biggest trading partners? What would Will have thought of "Operation Desert Storm"? It's hard to say.

Will was a world traveler, and his opinions were formed by going places and seeing things firsthand. There is little doubt he would have responded compassionately to the suffering and human rights abuses he would witness in our world today. But common sense would dictate that minding one's own business is much more difficult now than it was in Will's day. In a political climate where computers, mass communication, and supersonic transportation have generated weapons of mass destruction, spy satellites, and armies that can be mobilized in a heartbeat, Will would surely stand by his commitment to military preparedness. But, given the complexity of our world, it is hard to argue that everything Will had to say over sixty years ago would apply to the situations we face today. People in Will's time had fears of their own, but they did not include nuclear proliferation, international terrorism, or environmental degradation. When writing his columns, Will had no idea that scores of biographers, historians, and political scientists would be scrutinizing them for accuracy on into the next millennium. But even so, Will was an eminently practical man, and his common sense holds up very well. In the following comments, Will's views resonate with some of the trends we are seeing now. But beyond that, in addressing the issues of war and patriotism in his day, Will pointed to the human failings that have fueled nationalism and warfare throughout the ages. This morning's paper is graphic evidence that those same failings are still with us.

WAR

"I am a peace man. I haven't got any use for wars and there is no more humor in 'em than there is reason for 'em.[5]

"You know, if there is any excuse for anybody fighting at this time, it's beyond me. The consensus of opinion is that, 'so and so has to fight so and so sooner or later.' Well I believe if I had to fight a man 'sooner or later' I would fight him later, and the later the better. The only legitimate reason I can see why Germany and France must fight is they haven't fought in sixteen years, and the only reason I can see why us and Japan has to fight is because we haven't fought before.[6]

"Course I guess I am all wet, but I never have seen any reason why us, or any other nation, should hold under subjection of any kind, any islands or country outside of our own. We are going to get into a war some day either over Honolulu or the Philippines. So, let's all come home and let every nation ride its own surfboard, play its own eukaleles and commit their devilment on their own race.[7] *I mean, wouldn't it be wonderful if we ever live to see the day when any country can have its own revolution, or even a private and congenial war with a neighboring nation, without uninvited guests?*[8]

"Why, I told the Secretary of our Navy right from the stage the other night, that I wished we had the biggest Navy in the World, the biggest Army, and by all means the biggest Aeroplane force, but have it understood with the taxpayers that they are ONLY TO BE USED ON THE HOME GROUNDS. Now how in the world will you tell me is there a better way to prevent war than that. Be ready for it and stay at home. When they know they can't lick you, they certainly are not coming away over here to try it.[9]

"If you want to know when a war is coming, just watch the United States and see when they start cutting down on their defense. It's the surest barometer in the world.

"But you know, there will always be war. You got

every nation that's not in it boosting for it, for everybody makes money out of a war but the nations fighting. There is no industry under the sun you can get credit for as quick for as you can a war.[10]

"So it's pretty simple really, take the profits out of war, and you won't have any war.[11] *All in the world they got to do to stop it instantly is to agree to not trade with an aggressor nation, but they won't sacrifice their trade just to save bloodshed.*

"We've got the weapon to stop war, but try and get the nations to give up that trade. What's a few thousand dead compared to a cash customer?"[12]

Refusing to trade with an aggressor nation meant more than just cutting off their supply of bicycles, pencils, and chewing gum. A tremendous amount of money was being made selling the tools of war. Many industrialized nations had invested heavily in this lucrative business, and the United States was fast becoming the largest arms supplier in the world. As this trend developed, Will felt compelled to prick the conscience of the nation. Somebody had to.

"I see where we have the exclusive contract to furnish all ammunition for this and the next five wars in Mexico. That's a good idea. If you can't match a war yourself, why…get the contract to furnish the material for some other wars. You know, that's a great thing. You take a lot of nations and if they were not able to buy ammunition, why they just couldn't go to war. I tell you there is nothing in the world as disheartening to a country as to want to go to war and can't. So I think we are to be heartily commended for obliging a suffering humanity.[13]

"All our highly civilized nations are great humanitar-

ians. If two countries are going to kill each other off, neutrals at least would like the privilege of furnishing the ammunition. When the judgment day comes, civilization will have an alibi, 'I never took a human life, I only sold the fellow the gun to take it with.'[14]

"England tries to stop war, we try to stop disarmament. One fellow tries to stop the actual fight, we try to regulate the number of bullets he will have after the fight starts. Take your pick as to who is the humanitarian.[15]

"Why, asking Europe to disarm is like asking a man in Chicago to give up his life insurance. We can preach 'good-will,' but if we lived in Europe among those hyenas, we would be in a war before we got our grip unpacked.[16] *Take that Yugoslavia, they just seem to want to fight anyhow. Be a good joke on them if nobody prevented 'em.*[17]

"Well, here's another scheme for stopping war. It's this…no nation is allowed to enter a war till they have paid for the last one."[18]

One of the major criticisms of our current "all-volunteer army" is that, if we were to go to war, it is possible that mostly poor and lower-middle class kids would end up doing all the dying. What is the motivation for young college graduates, with opportunities in the job market, to join the service? Or consider the sons and daughters of the wealthy. With their schooling and financial futures almost guaranteed, are they more or less inclined to volunteer to get shot at? The ranks of our services have a large number of enlistees for whom the service is their only escape from poverty. It is a wonderful thing that the military can provide these young people with a chance to improve their lot in life. But is it really fair that only they should be on the front lines when the suffering starts, while the more privileged of us watch it on television?

Will had a few suggestions that would not only make things a lot fairer, but just might put an end to war altogether.

DRAFT WEALTH

"Here's an idea. Mr. Harding had this idea and I thought it was a good one. His idea was the conscription of all wealth in case of war. It would be a very interesting experiment and would add novelty to the next war.[19]

"Here's how it would work; When that Wall Street Millionaire knows that you are not only going to come into his office and take his Secretary and Clerks, but that you will come in to get his dough too, say, boy, there wouldn't be any war.

"You will hear the question: 'yes, but how could you do it?'

"Say, you take a boy's life, don't you? When you take boys away, you take everything they have in the world, that is, their life. You send them to war and what part of that life you don't use, you let him come back with it. Perhaps you may use all of it. Well, that's the way to do with wealth. Take all he has, give him a bare living the same as you do the Soldier. Give him the same allowance as the soldier...all of us that stay at home. The government should own everything we have, use what it needs to conduct the whole expenses of the war, and give back what is left, if there is any, the same as you give back to the boy what he has left.

"There can be no profiteering. The government owns everything till the war is over. Every man, woman, and child, from Henry Ford and John D. down, get their dol-

lar and a quarter a day the same as the soldier. The only way a man could profiteer in a war like that would be to raise more children.

"But, no, it will never get anywhere. The rich will say it ain't practical, and the poor will never get a chance to find out if it is or not."[20]

Will Rogers from *A Connecticut Yankee in King Arthur's Court*

On a more serious note, Will said the following,

> *"I believe that a child could prevent all wars. Let a Congress, or a Reichstag, or a Parliament, or a House of Deputies be on the verge of breaking off diplomatic relations with some other country, and you let a child enter that Chamber and say: 'What about me? What is to become of us? We have no say. Are not you men smart enough and generous enough to settle this without war? It won't hurt you. We are the sufferers; it will leave us fatherless; and after we grow up we will have the debt to pay, so please think twice before breaking off relations, and are you sure that it can't be prevented?' There is no truer line in our entire Scripture than, 'A little child shall lead them.'*[21]
>
> *"But ya know, people talk peace, but men give their life's work to war. It won't stop till there is as much brains and scientific study put to aid peace as there is to promote war.* [22] *Still, even if you get peace you gotta remember, peace is kinder like prosperity. There is mighty few nations that can stand it."*[23]

MINDIN' OUR OWN BUSINESS

Will spent much of his time and newspaper space cautioning us about getting too overzealous in promoting our way of life around the world. Regarding missionaries, he once said, *"All the Missionaries in the world can't make China Presbyterian. My theory of the whole Missionary business could be summed up in a sentence. If you send somebody to teach somebody, be sure that the system you are teaching is better than the system they are practicing. Some think it is, some think it ain't. A difference of opinion is what makes horse racing and Missionaries."*[24]

In the mid-thirties, Will saw others persuading their neighbors by force of arms and said, *"Japan wants a 'Monroe Doctrine' now, with them playing the part of Monroe, doctoring on China. Not only 'doctoring,' but operating.*[25] *But you know, Japan, you got to admire 'em. They are so ambitious, and they just got everything that all the other nations have but a sense of humor."*[26] Will didn't trust what he saw coming from Nazi Germany either. *"Papers all state Hitler is trying to copy Mussolini. Looks to me like it's the Ku Klux that he is copying. He don't want to be Emperor, he wants to be Kleagle."*[27]

Although Will traveled extensively in Europe and Asia, politically, he just watched them from afar. He thought it unwise for the United States to get mired in the affairs of other warring nations. His advice to President Roosevelt was, *"Mr. Franklin D., shut your front door to all foreign ambassadors running to you with news. Just send 'em these words: 'Boys, it's your cats that's fighting, you pull 'em apart.'"*[28]

In the early 1930s, Europe and Asia were fertile ground for tyranny. Nationalism took root in the fear, anger, and economic desperation of the people. Extremists simply had to identify the "enemy" in the public's mind and then pervert the idea of patriotism to their ends. Once they had patriotism on one side and the "enemy" on the other, they could easily do away with anyone who criticized their ultranationalistic vision.

Will was instinctively opposed to such manipulation. He resisted any form of political litmus testing. Some politicians started promoting such testing long before the turmoil of the '30s led to World War II. As early as 1927, in the wake of the Red Scare, Will saw our nation leaning in a nationalistic direction. He thought the trend was exemplified by the mayor of Chicago, "Big Bill" Thompson, and his "America First Society." In an effort to nip this type of thinking in the bud, Will skewered Mr. Thompson with the following comment in his daily telegram.

"Mayor Bill Thompson of Chicago has started a society called 'America First.' You send $10 to defray the expenses of trying to keep it 'first.' Bill has the nucleus of a good idea, but, like any good idea, it's the improvements that make it.

"So I hereby offer stock in a society called 'America Only' at $20 a share. Why be only first? Let's be the whole thing. Why spend $10 to be in front when $10 more will put you in front, behind and in the middle all at the same time? If everybody in America will give me $20, I will be more than glad to show them where we are the 'only nation in the world.' Besides, this money will not all revert to me. A small percentage will be spent in exterminating all other nations.

"Who'll be the first to display super-patriotism and join 'America Only' ?"[29]

Just to make sure his message wasn't misunderstood, Will decided to elaborate on his "America Only" concept in his next weekly article. It is always fun to read someone's work when they are truly on a roll, and that is the feeling here. Far ahead of his time, Will latched on to the multicultural identity of America and issued what amounted to nothing short of a broadside.

SUPER-PATRIOTISM

"There has been a terrible lot of various Societys formed to try and instill Americanism into our lagging

Patriots. If you have never formed a Society in your life and don't know what to form one about, why don't let that worry you in the least. Just start to sponsor 'Better Citizenship,' or '100 percent Americanism,' 'America for the Americans,' or any of those original ideas. There has been quite an epidemic of these, especially since the war.

"It seems that before the war come along, we were really kinder lax in our duty toward declaring just what we were. The war come along and about all we could do was to muster up five or six million men of every breed and color that ever been invented. Now these poor fellows didn't know whether they were '100 percent Americans' or 'Better Citizens,' or what they were, and we started them drilling so fast that they didn't have time to go through a clinic and find out.

"You see up to then they didn't know what all this meant. They thought that as long as they paid their taxes, tended to their own business, went to their own churches, kept kinder within the law, that that was all they was supposed to do. And it was like that in the old days. But you see, we was a backwards nation and didn't know it.

"What we had to learn was to be better Americans. Why here was old men that had raised a big family and had never said 'America First.' Can you imagine such ignorance? How they had ever been able to do this without declaring where they stood was just another one of our lucky blunders. So when the war come along and we found out that all everybody would do was to die, or suffer, or get rich (or whatever the circumstances called for) for their country, why we saw right away that something was needed to instill patriotism. So hence the forming of all these various societies. They come just in the nick of

time. For after the war, a lot of young men, who had never known much about other men from different parts of the country, and different nationalities, they had, during the days in camps and in France, become to know and like and understand each other, and find out each other's viewpoint.

"In other words, it was just the start of what might a been a bad friendship and understanding. But it's like everything else, when the necessity arises somebody always arises with the remedy. So, on investigation it was found that a lot of these same boys were not 100 percent Americans at all. We had been kinder lax in who we had let into our war, everything had come up so hurriedly. Why a lot of them couldn't even speak English. A lot of them didn't go to churches, in fact, there was a million things we found out that we should have found out before we associated with 'em. Of course it was all too late now and was all over, and we would just have to charge it off to bad management. But let's get organized and don't let it happen again. We all went in 50/50 in war time, but this is peace now and we got time to see who is who and why.

"So these Societys commenced to be formed and they grabbed our little civilization just when it was on the brink and hauled it back to normalcy. You see in America there was originally just one Society (well, it was really two combined): it was the Declaration of Independence, and the Constitution of the United States. If you was here and belonged to that, why you was all members of the same Club. You didn't know whether you was 100 percent, or 2 and 3/4 percent, or what ratio you was. You didn't know whether you was a good citizen or bad one. All you knew was that you belonged to this club called America, and all you had to do was work for it, fight for

it and act like a gentleman, that was all the bylaws there was. As long as you did that, you could worship what you wanted to, talk any language you wanted to, in fact it looked like a pretty liberal layout. But after 150 or more years, it was immediately seen that this plan was no good, that the old boys that layed out the Constitution didn't know much. That the country should be divided up in various Societys and Cliques. So that brings us down to this generation, who really are showing us just what to do to prove that we are not against the old Fatherland.

"We used to think that we were for it, as long as we didn't do anything against it, but now we find we got to join something and announce daily that we are for it. We have got to weed out the ones that are not 100 percent. We got to get around these luncheons more, and sing some get-together songs.

"So you see it's stuff like that that will save us. If those kind of clubs and societys hadn't been formed just when they was, this would have been a fine looking country now. So get into a club as soon as you can. I don't care what it is, just so it's banded together to make somebody else's life miserable and yours great.

"Now if you don't belong to some of these Clubs or societies, why the first thing you know you will be getting narrow minded enough to want to give everybody an even break regardless of everything.

"Now, I have looked over all the clubs and none of them seem to have enough scope, or broad minded ideal. 'America First' is all right, but it allows somebody else to be second. Now sometimes a thing that's second can be almost as good as something that's first. So that's the thing my Society avoids. It's with the whole idea of there being no one else. In other words, I am just taking the

spirit and foundation of other clubs and societys and making them broader.

"They are against something. (They got to be against something or they wouldn't be formed.) Well, mine improves on any of theirs…it's against everything. I can take my 'America Only' idea and eliminate wars. The minute we extinguish all other nations there will be no more wars, unless it's a civil war among ourselves, and that of course we can take care of right here at home. I am getting a lot of applications already…real red-blooded go-gettum Americans, that have seen this country trampled under foreign feet enough. Why I figure the patriotism in my organization, when I get it formed, will run around 165 or 170 percent American. It will make a sucker out of these little 100 percent organizations. It's not too late to send your $20 yet. Remember when you belong to 'America Only' you are the last word in organizations."[30]

Will Rogers – Honorary Mayor of Beverly Hills

Will gave Mayor Thompson a hard time but he was once a mayor of sorts himself. In 1926, Will was appointed "Honorary Mayor of Beverly Hills." In accepting the honor he said, *"They say I'll be a comedy mayor. Well, I won't be the only one. I never saw a mayor that wasn't comical. As to my administration, I won't say I'll be exactly honest, but I'll agree to split 50-50 with you and give the town an even break. I'm for the common people, and as Beverly Hills has no common people I won't have to pass out any favors."*[31] Will was so popular in 1930 that an article in *American Magazine* stated, "You can never have another war in this country unless Will Rogers is for it."

Apparently Chicago's mayor was one of the few people ever to challenge Will's popularity publicly. On another occasion, in the depth of the depression, "Big Bill" took great offense when Will teased him in a column about his Thompson Lottery Plan. The Mayor was voted out of office in the next election and the word on the street was that his lack of being a good sport contributed to his defeat.

5

CANNIBALS, LOAN SHARKS, AND BUSINESSMEN

It is hard to believe but there is a terrible prejudice running rampant in this nation – "Wealthism." Regardless of their race, creed, or gender, if they're rich, we don't like 'em. We are envious of them because they have more stuff than we do. And, as you know, the name of the game these days is, "Get More Stuff." We must confess that there are times when we look at some of our well-heeled brethren and sistren and doubt that there are human beings residing behind all of that power and influence. Regardless, I am here to say (and I know this is a revolutionary idea) that there are those among the wealthy who deserve membership in our club (the human race), even though most of us can't afford to belong to any of theirs. I can hear some of you protesting. But in my travels, I have met more than a few wealthy people who were "regular birds" at heart.

Will spent a lot of time in the company of lawyers, bankers, and businessmen. He treated these rich fellows the same way he treated the old cowpokes he chatted with across the back fence – and they liked him for it. Will had a playfulness that cut right through people's stations in life and went straight to their humanity. He made fun of people like Henry Ford, John D. Rockefeller, and Presidents Calvin Coolidge and Franklin Roosevelt. For the most part, they all took it in stride and considered Will a personal friend. But there were times when a few of his targets got miffed. Although Will liked to keep harmony with his public, his love of having friends never prevented him from "calling 'em like he saw 'em." He said, *"The one thing I am proud of is the fact that there is not a man in public life today that I don't like. Most of them are my good friends, but that's not going to keep me from taking a dig at him when he does something or says something foolish."*[1]

LAWYERS

If you think lawyer jokes are something new, think again. Not only were lawyers one of Will's favorite targets, but taking shots at the legal profession has always been considered good sport. Even the lawyers themselves have come to accept the fact that being in the legal profession makes them fair game for comedians and commentators. I was under the impression that even the Bard took shots at lawyers. But one of the most frequently quoted Shakespearean statements, "First thing we do, let's kill all the lawyers," from Henry VI, was actually intended as high praise – a compliment to the legal profession. David T. Link, Dean of the University of Notre Dame Law School points out that, in the context of the story, Shakespeare's lawyers were the only group that stood in the way of two evil characters who were planning a revolution through which they could eventually take away the rights and property of the citizenry. In fact, Link points out, history shows that a despot's first move has always been "to subordinate the rule of law and the legal profession."[2]

So the questions arise: How could lawyers go from being seen as the guardians of our rights and property to hired guns, selling their services to the highest bidder? And why is the legal profession now rated somewhere below Congress in the public eye? According to Mr. Link, the American Bar Association found that "...the primary reason for this lack of trust is the belief by many that lawyers lack ethics." He further states that focusing on morality and ethics, while reforming the way law is taught and practiced, is the best way to change that perception.

The American Bar Association's revelation is not news to most of us – nor would it be news to Will. Regarding ethics, Will said, *"Bar associations invented the word 'ethics,' then forgot about it."*[3] Will wasn't convinced you could reform lawyers any more than you could reform politicians. He said, *"Personally I don't think you can make a lawyer honest by an act of the Legislature. You've got to work on his conscience. And his lack of conscience is what makes him a lawyer."*[4] Maybe he saw lawyers and politicians as one and the same thing. Regarding one-term presidents, he quipped, *"A man don't any more than learn where the Ice Box is in the White House than he has to go back to being a lawyer again."*[5]

Will considered lawyers fundamentally decent and well intended. But as a comedian, he couldn't resist the treasure trove of foibles and contradictions they offered him. He took great delight in playfully taunting the legal profession, as he did in his

STRANGE TALE OF A HARVARD CANNIBAL

"In a Sunday article I stated that the Donner Party was our only cannibalism. I was wrong, as usual, for I just learned of this case.

"Crossing the divide from Utah to Colorado in 1872, a man named Packer evidently practiced it. He was convicted in Del Norte, Colorado, and the judge passed sentence as follows:

"'Packer, you have committed the worlds most fiendish crime. You not only murdered your companions, but you ate up every Democrat in Hillsdale County. You are to hang by the neck till you are dead, and may God have mercy on your Republican soul.'[6]

"Now if ol' Packer had just eaten up a Republican, why the Judge, (a fine old high type Democrat from Arkansaw) would have perhaps given the man a pension instead of a sentence. Well, now we got that much straight.

"I suppose, a lot of you folks might think I am just kidding about this Packer, and the story of the Democrats but it is the gospel truth. I certainly wouldn't make light of a thing so serious as eating a Democrat.

"Now, here is the things I want you to get. It's the history of this fellow Packer before he started in subsisting on the minority party. Packer was a Harvard Graduate, and graduated in '66. He was a Law Student and started practicing in Boston. What I am getting at is that the only case of a person willfully devouring human flesh was by the Alumni of the great Harvard. So Harvard has not only produced the least understandable English in our fair land, but produced the only living Cannibal.

Then, he was a Lawyer. That of course seems natural, their profession is an offshoot of the cannibal profession. They generally skin 'em alive. Packer did have the good taste to destroy 'em and get 'em out of their misery. Most Lawyers delight in seeing their victims suffer.

"It was the winter of '72 and '73. There was six Companions, and they were all well equipped with provisions. But in the snow they got lost from their Burros. It was the first time, and perhaps the last that a Lawyer was ever permitted to accompany a band of Prospectors

into the mountains. He always waits till they go out and find it, and then he gets his share by showing 'em where to sign their name. But Packer was afraid they would come back and find another Lawyer, so he just went along with 'em.

"Well it seems there was dissension from the start in that he claimed he overheard them [the prospectors] plotting to kill and eat him. But that didn't go with the Judge and Jury. They knew no man could ever be so hungry that they would eat a Lawyer.

"Now I was wrong in one little misstatement about the case, I had heard that he was hung. He was not. Colorado was then a Territory and the game laws did not protect Democrats. Even to this day in some States it would not be considered illegal to eat one. So they give him forty years in Canyon City Jail. That was a little over six years for each one he ate. You would have to eat at least ten or more to get life according to Colorado justice. He didn't stay in there that long. Along in '99, when Civilization and the Denver Post hit us, why them and other papers started a campaign to release him. There was a tight election coming on, and them being Republicans, they wanted to let him out hoping he would eat up some more Democrats before November 4th.

"Then they brought up that the Judge, had been biased in the trial, that no Democratic Judge should sit in a case, where it was Democrats that had been eaten. The Editorials of the Denver Papers of that time all brought out this injustice. That it was a blot on the fair name of Colorado that a Harvard man shouldn't be able to eat what he liked. Well, anyhow, the papers got him out, and the fair name of Colorado was saved, and since then they have never convicted, or even tried a man, for murdering,

> *robbing or otherwise maiming a Democrat. Viva Democracy!*
>
> *"Oh Yes! I forgot to tell you he was the Son of a missionary, and in his youth had spent some time in the South Sea Islands. That's how he acquired this taste. A Missionary, a Lawyer, a Harvard Graduate, I want to tell you, Illiteracy is a blessing."*[7]

The "Harvard Cannibal" was a good-natured lark. In other articles, you get the sense that Will was downright fed up with the shenanigans of the legal industry. Sometimes he laid it on pretty heavy.

> *"Just by way of warning, I have always noticed that any time a man can't come and settle with you without bringing his lawyer, why, look out for him."* [8]
>
> *"Did you read how many thousands of students just graduated all over the country in law? Going to take an awful lot of crime to support that bunch.*
>
> *"Now, a man naturally pulls for the business that brings him in his living. That's just human nature. So look what a new gang we got assisting devilment, all trained to get a guilty man out on a technicality and an innocent one in on their opposing lawyer's mistake. This is the heyday of the shyster lawyer and they defend each other for half rates."* [9]

Comments as strong as that one got some people in the profession riled up. In 1935, some attorneys took offense when Will spoke at the Convention of the American Bar Association in Los Angeles. As you can tell by his Daily Telegram the next day, the audience didn't receive him all that well. *"Went down and spoke at some lawyers' meeting last night. They didn't* *think much of my little squib yesterday about driving the shysters out of their profession. They seemed to kinder doubt just who would have to leave. Pretty serious, some of `em. But the big percentage are regular guys."*[10]

While addressing the group, Will was reported to have said that the dominant question at the convention should be: *"Before the criminal is tried, the defense consul should stand trial to see if there was anything against him [the attorney]."* Shortly thereafter, an editorialist in one of the profession's publications made such a stink about the incident that Will felt compelled to issue a rebuttal in his weekly article. Parts of Will's response went as follows:

> *"Well now, let's take up the issues one by one. In the first place if there had been no truth at all in the statement I made there would never have been any yell about it. Now, as to it being the dominant question, Mr. Rogers didn't say that it was the dominant question, he said that it should be the dominant question. In other words the lawyers would give their eye teeth to have the thing cleaned up, and they will admit that it would be of more benefit to their profession to have the crooks driven out than to have done any other thing.*
>
> *"Now here is a thing. I am in the movies. When there was so much talk of cleaning up the movies, there wasn't a lawyer, or any other profession but what said, 'Why don't they clean those things up? My wife and children can't go to see 'em.'*
>
> *"Now you offered an opinion in my business, but the minute a comedian offers an opinion in your business, I am out of place. Your business is sacred and no one should mention it only in the highest terms. Say, lawyers is everybody's business the same as the movies are.*

"Get this one: 'There was a time a few years back when a dig at the lawyers at the Bijou Theater was a sure fire laugh, but now the so-called humorists have sensed the distastes in the mouths of the public for such efforts of humor.' Well I wish he could have read a 'so-called humorist's' mail. Never did I have so much approving mail on one article, and not a half dozen dissenting ones, and they were from lawyers. Every layman approved. It batted about 98 per cent. I wish I could think of something else as true and as good.

"Some of my very best friends are lawyers, and are yet. But they don't think their fraternity is some almighty deity. The biggest part of the lawyers are regular guys, the same as most of them are honest and high type in their profession. But they know there is undesirable among them, and they are not going to faint when it's mentioned.

"If this old boy don't think that the audience will still laugh at the lawyers at the Bijou Theatre, just let him book me for a lecture on lawyers at the Bijou, and come and sit and listen to 'em roar. The banker, the lawyer, and the politician are still our best bets for a laugh. Audiences haven't changed at all, and neither has the three above professions. And incidentally, comedians haven't improved. Nothing has improved but taxes."[11]

Will didn't usually get involved in this kind of squabbling with people over a difference of opinion. But perhaps the combination of not being that well received when speaking to the group, followed by an unfriendly review in their publication, was just a little too much. Lawyers and doctors are similar in that we complain about them until one of them comes along and saves our skin. Then, although we're greatly relieved, we still hate to pay them for their services. Will knew this. But he wasn't about to roll over for someone who couldn't take a joke. He summed up his approach this way, *"You can always joke about a big Man that is really big, But don't ever kid about the little fellow that thinks he is something, cause he will get sore. That's why he's little."*[12]

Will called himself a comedian but he insisted that he was not just a gag artist. He said he preferred it when he could get you to nudge a friend and say, "You know, he's right about that." He said he liked that a lot better than if you laughed real loud and then, a couple of minutes later, forgot what it was that you were laughing at. So Will was just as much a philosopher as he was a comedian. His gift for taking a serious subject and bringing a little lightness to it made his comments operate on two levels. They were humorous, yet there was an underlying seriousness that provided food for thought. He explained by saying, *"I claim you have to have a serious streak in you or you can't see the funny side in the other fellow."*[13]

Much of the time Will's humor came out of a playful effort to make sense of human behavior. Here, Will tries to explain lawyers and their "racket." I suppose his explanation is as good as anyone's.

> *"The minute you read something and you can't understand it you can almost be sure that it was drawn up by a lawyer. Then if you give it to another lawyer to read and he don't know just what it means, why then you can be sure it was drawn up by a lawyer. If it's in a few words and is plain and understandable only one way, it was written by a non-lawyer.*
>
> *"Every time a lawyer writes something, he is not writing for posterity, he is writing so that endless others of his*

craft can make a living out of trying to figure out what he said. Course perhaps he hadn't really said anything, that's what makes it hard to explain.[14]

"Take wills for example. Modern History has proven that there has never yet been a will left that was carried out exactly as the maker of the money intended. So if you are thinking of dying and have any money, I would advise you to leave the following will: 'Count up the Lawyers in the State and divide it among them. If there should by any miracle be any left, let my Relatives, all of them, God Bless 'em, fight over it.'

"If it wasn't for Wills, lawyers would have to go to work at an essential employment. There is only one way you can beat a Lawyer in a death case. That is to die with nothing. Then you can't get a Lawyer within 10 miles of your house.[15]

"Anyhow, they are like a lot more of the crafts that many of us live by, great but useless. But Lord if we go into the things that are useless, why two thirds of the world would have to turn to manual labor. That's really the only essential thing there is, anyhow."[16]

Will came by his ability to make fun of the rich and powerful honestly. He cut his teeth on the sophisticates that made up his Ziegfeld Follies audiences in the 1920s. Speaking to dignitaries and wealthy industrialists at their special functions became as natural to him as addressing the local chamber of commerce. He developed his very relaxed and personable style by thinking of his audience as his friends. This remained a hallmark of his approach in the years to come.

The political and business climate in those early days was quite conservative. Looking back on the '20s today, we can point to many social injustices. The country was a study in extremes. There were terrible working conditions for many workers and a tremendous gap between the rich and the poor. By making fun of influential politicians, organized crime, prohibition, Wall Street, and the wealthy, Will endeared himself to king and commoner alike.

Will hobnobbin' with the "Big Boys"

Will's speech to the Bankers Association in 1922 provides an excellent example of his bravado when approaching a wealthy audience. He pulled out all the stops, and they just loved it. They invited him back to "abuse" them year after year. Perhaps they were making so much money at the time that they felt they could afford to laugh at themselves.

BANKERS SPEECH

"Ladies and Gentlemen! Honored guests...loan sharks and interest hounds! I have addressed every form of organized graft in the U.S., excepting Congress. So, it's

naturally a pleasure for me to appear before the biggest.

"You are without a doubt, the most disgustingly rich audience I ever talked to, with the possible exception of the Bootleggers Union, Local 1, combined with the enforcement officers.

"Now I understand you hold this convention every year to announce what the annual gyp will be. I have often wondered where the depositors hold their convention. I see where your convention was opened by a prayer, and you had to send outside your ranks to get somebody that could pray. You should have had one creditor here, he would have shown you how to pray!

"I noticed that in the prayer the clergyman announced to the Almighty that the bankers were here. Well, it wasn't exactly an announcement, it was more in the nature of a warning. He didn't tell the devil, he figured the devil knew where you were all the time.

"I see by your speeches that you are very optimistic of the business condition of the coming year. If I had your dough, I would be optimistic, too.

"Will you please tell me what you do with all the vice presidents a bank has? I guess that's to get you more discouraged before you can see the president. Why, the United States is the biggest business institution in the world, and they only have one vice president, and nobody has ever found anything for him to do.

"I have met most of you, as I come out of the stage door of the Follies every night. I want to tell you that any of you that are capitalized under a million dollars, needn't hang around out there. Our girls may not know their Latin and Greek, but they certainly know their Dunn and Bradstreet.

"You have a wonderful organization. I understand

you have ten thousand here tonight, and with what you have in the various federal prisons, that brings your membership up to around thirty thousand.

"So, good-bye paupers, you are the finest bunch of Shylocks that ever foreclosed a mortgage on a widow's home." [17]

As you can see, Will could land his barbs pretty close to home. But, when speaking before a group, he never stepped over the line from kidding into attacking his hosts. His columns, by contrast, afforded him greater leeway. They could have more of an edge. Will wouldn't attack individuals. But he would criticize a group and its policies, usually adding a little self-effacing remark at the end – just to be fair.

"Why, the Chinese as a race have forgot more honesty, and gentlemanliness than we will ever know if we live another Century. If a Bank fails in China they behead the men at the head of it that was responsible. If one fails over here, we write the men up in the Magazines, as how 'They started poor, worked hard, took advantage of their opportunities, (and Depositors) and today they are rated as 'up in the millions.'[18]

"If you think it ain't a Sucker Game, why is your Banker the richest man in your Town? Why is your Bank the biggest and finest building in your Town?

"You will say, well, what will all the Bankers do? I don't care what they do. Let 'em go to work, if there is any job any of them could earn a living at. Banking and After Dinner Speaking are two of the most Non-essential industries we have in this country. I am ready to reform if they are."[19]

Although he could lean on these old boys pretty hard, he

had a rule that he wouldn't make fun of people when they were down. These comments were made during the Roaring Twenties when the bankers were riding high. Will figured they could afford to have a little of the air taken out of them. But after the stock market crashed in 1929 and some of the same men who were in his audiences had jumped out of tall buildings after losing their fortunes, Will tempered his comments. He didn't gloat on anyone's misery. Although he was still critical of the mistakes made by the banking industry, he went on to make fun of people who were in a better position to laugh at their situation.

BUSINESSMEN

And make fun he did. In Richard M. Ketchum's classic biography, *Will Rogers – The Man and His Times,* the author relates how Will would grab the attention of his after-dinner audiences by opening his speeches with an insult. According to Ketchum, Will called a group of automobile dealers, *"old time Horse trading Gyps with white collars on."* Advertising men were the *"Robbing Hoods of America."* He told the Association of Woolen Men not to get caught in the rain or there would be *"about 500 men choked to death by their own suits."*[20]

Will made fun of lawyers, bankers, and businessmen, but at heart he admired people who got things done. He praised men of accomplishment from Mahatma Ghandi to John D. Rockefeller; Knute Rockne to Charles A. Lindbergh – and women, too, like Amelia Earhart, Lady Astor, and Eleanor Roosevelt. Regardless of their field of endeavor, Will liked winners. With his tongue in cheek, he showed his basic admiration for Henry Ford when he said,

"I launched a Ford for President movement... We ain't

going to have any party. It's to be called the 'All over the Road Party' with Mr. Ford for leader. Our slogan will be 'Come with Ford and you will at least get somewhere.' I would love to see Mr. Ford in there, really. I don't know who started the idea that a President must be a Politician instead of a Business man. A Politician can't run any other kind of business. So there is no reason why he can run the U.S. That's the biggest single business in the World.

"I just would love to see Mr. Ford, when Congress pulled one of those long stalls of theirs, going around and lifting up the hood and seeing what is the matter." [21]

ADVERTISING

In our age of sound bites, the one-line slogan rules. Slogans such as, "Just Do It!," "It's the Real Thing!," and "The Heartbeat of America" all bring their companies products to mind without ever mentioning their names. Every good business executive knows that whether you're creating an idea, a product or a candidate, it always boils down to a marketing problem. But is it possible that we have taken this marketing thing a little too far? What would Will Rogers, coming from simpler times, think of the advertising overload that the average American is subject to these days?

- Phone calls from telemarketers at dinnertime.
- Radio advertisers who shout at their listeners.
- TV infomercials passing as entertainment.
- Landscapes covered with billboards.

Along with a chicken in every pot, we've got a "franchise row" in every town. Will lamented this creeping commercialization of America as far back as 1929. He said, *"We've started building our towns alike: Filling Stations on two corners and Drug Stores on the other two. You can pick up a block out of any town in America and sneak in and put it down in the night in another town, and it will be a month before anybody notices the difference."*[22]

What would Will think of a society that not only endures all of this incessant advertising but also participates in it by offering up their bodies as advertising space? He would have to find it humorous that we will pay premium prices for T-shirts, beach towels, ball caps, and luggage that advertise soft drinks, vacation spots, mutual funds, cartoon shows, beer, sports teams, cigarettes, suntan lotion, health clubs, movies, bottled water, and snuff.

As you will see, Mr. Rogers was fed up with advertising slogans way back when Madison Avenue was in its infancy. We can only guess what he would think of it all today.

> *"Everything nowadays is a Saying, or Slogan. You can't go to bed, you can't get up, you can't brush your Teeth without doing it to some Advertising Slogan. We are even born nowadays by a Slogan: 'Better Parents have Better Babies.' Our Children are raised by a Slogan: 'Feed your Baby Cowlicks Malted Milk and he will be another Dempsey.' Everything is a Slogan and of all the Bunk things in America the Slogan is the Champ. There never was one that lived up to its name. They can't manufacture a new Article until they have a Slogan to go with it. You can't form a new Club unless it has a catchy Slogan. The merits of the thing has nothing to do with it. It is, just how good is the Slogan?*
> *Congress even has Slogans:*
> *'Why sleep at home when you can sleep in Congress?'*
> *'Be a politician – no training necessary.'*
> *'It is easier to fool 'em in Washington than it is at home, So why not be a Senator.'*

'Come to Washington and vote to raise your own pay.'

"All such Slogans are held up to the youth of this Country. You can't sit down in a Street Car after a hard day's work without having a Slogan staring you in the face.

"The Prize one of all is: 'Two can live as cheap as one.' That, next to law enforcement, is the biggest Bunk Slogan ever invented. Two can't even live as cheap as two, much less one.

"Then the Preachers say: 'Let no man put asunder.' And two-thirds of the married World is asunder in less than three months.

"Then comes the Furniture Slogan: 'A dollar down and a Dollar a week.' It's few wives that last with the same husband until the cook Stove is paid for.

"'It's cheaper to buy than pay rent.' Half the people in the United States are living on interest paid by people who will never get the last mortgage paid out.

"We even got into the War on a Slogan that was supposed to keep us out. After we got in we were going to 'Make the world safe for Democracy.' and maybe we did – you can't tell, because there is no Nation ever tried Democracy since.

"P.T. Barnum come nearer having a true Slogan than anybody; 'There is a Sucker born every minute.'

"You see, a fool Slogan can get you into anything. But you never heard of a Slogan getting you out of anything. It takes either Bullets, Hard Work or Money to get you out of anything. Nobody has ever invented a Slogan to use instead of paying your Taxes.

"But they will fall for 'em. You shake a Slogan at an American and it's just like showing a hungry Dog a Bone. We even die by Slogans. I saw an Undertaker's sign the

other day which read: 'There is a satisfaction in dying if you know the Woodlawn Brothers are to bury you.'"[23]

6

MEDIA MAGIC AND MODESTY

"Betty is to blame for it all. Whatever I am, or have accomplished, I owe to Betty. I ain't got no sense: my wife made me what I am."[1]

Jim Rogers once said of his mother, "If you knew my mother, you would understand Betty Blake was the reason there was a Will Rogers.[2] Although Dad was a perfectionist, and a man who worked very hard and drove himself very hard, he needed Mother as his balance wheel, as someone to more or less show him the way. Once he got started he was tireless, but I know that a great deal of what he did developed from what she saw he was capable of. She was his anchor, she was also his severest critic....the old saying that 'Behind every great man stands a great woman' was certainly never truer than in the case of my Mother and Dad."[3]

Betty Blake was of humble origins. She came from a highly respected small-town family, but not a wealthy one. Her father ran a small lumber and grist mill in the little town of Silver Springs, Arkansas (later known as Monte Ne). He died when she was three. Shortly thereafter, she and her family moved into nearby Rogers, where her mother supported them by becoming a dressmaker. The Blake household, with its seven girls and two boys, was a center of social activity in town. The Blake kids were talented and fun-loving. Betty played banjo, mandolin, and piano, and she frequently sang and acted at the local Opera House.

While all of this was fun, the financial demands of a family of ten put Betty into the work force at an early age. Like Will, she did not finish high school, but she was a capable worker with a good head for business. Before marrying, she worked for the H. L. Stroud Mercantile Company, the *Rogers Democrat,* and the Frisco Railroad Station. But her business savvy was never as fully employed as it was later on, when she helped in managing her husband's career.

Betty was Will's trusted friend, lover, and confidant. He would have been lost without her. She prompted him to go out on the lecture circuit and into radio. Gentle but honest in her assessment of his writing and performing capabilities, she helped him with his columns and in choosing movie scripts that best suited him. While shepherding his career and maintaining a household, she also shouldered the day-to-day responsibilities of raising three children to adulthood. Being gone so much, Will knew how challenging Betty's role must have been. He reflected on his own mother and Betty's superior parenting skills this way,

> *"My own mother died when I was ten years old. My folks have told me that what little humor I have comes from her. I can't remember her humor but I can remember her love and her understanding of me. Of course, the mother I know the most about is the mother of our little group. She has been for twenty-two years trying to raise to maturity four children, three by birth and one by marriage. While she hasn't done a good job, the poor soul has done all that mortal human could do with the material she has had to work with."* [4]

Coming from hearty stock, both Will and Betty were

highly independent people. Most couples married young in those days, but they were both twenty-nine years old before they finally tied the knot. Their independent natures allowed them to endure separation while maintaining complete devotion to each other. Of the many historians who have looked at Will's life, all have found his commitment to Betty unwavering. So much so that once, while shooting a movie scene that required a kiss from the actress playing the role of his wife, Will was caught off guard. He had been avoiding shooting the scene for some time, until finally the director told the actress, Irene Rich, to wait until the appropriate moment and plant the kiss on him. Afterward, Will blushed and said that it made him feel as if he had been unfaithful to his wife.

As for Will's fathering ability, he confessed to being a lax disciplinarian. He left most of that to Betty, preferring to be more of a pal to his kids. But according to both Will Jr. and Jim, their father took his parenting quite seriously. When he was home, he was a full-time dad, giving his children loads of attention, playing just as hard as they did. Their ranch in Santa Monica was set up ideally for the family's constant riding, roping, and horseplay. When Will was away, he wrote the children often, especially his daughter, Mary. But this independent streak seemed to be a family trait. When I asked Will Jr. whether his father's being gone so much was a problem, Bill replied, "It was just the way things were. We all had very active lives. Dad was gone a lot. But he made up for it when he was home." Even though Will's travel demands had to be hard on family life, Betty and the kids accepted them as part of the package.

Being seen throughout the country and the world was to Will's advantage. His high visibility in the media propelled him to a level of recognition previously unknown in the entertainment industry. Entertainers in the nineteenth century were limited to the followings they could generate through public appearances. Will could touch more people with a single column, movie, or radio broadcast than those old performers could reach in a lifetime. He became a household name all across the country. With his roots in the Indian Territory and his simple country upbringing, he must have found this overwhelming at times. He saw himself as extremely lucky and explained the phenomenon by saying, *"I am just an old country boy in a big town trying to get along. I have been eating pretty regular, and the reason I have been is because I have stayed an old country boy."*[5]

Will's self-effacing nature and shy demeanor was not an act. In his early career, his posture on stage was marked by a characteristic slouch, his hands in his pockets or spinning a rope, a wad of chewing gum in his mouth, his hat tilted back on his head, and his eyes slightly lowered. While making his commentary, he would glance alternately between his audience and the floor. It was reminiscent of his first encounters with Betty. But as his career developed, Will could be seen speaking with more authority and confidence. No dummy, he learned early on that his natural reserve was at the root of his charm. He developed a style that let his audience see that he was struggling to overcome his shyness in order to perform. This gave them a sense of commonality with him and translated beautifully into newspaper columns, radio programs, motion pictures, and public appearances. In those arenas, he was comfortable and outgoing. But getting at what was underneath Will's public persona was more difficult.

According to Richard M. Ketchum, there was a private side to Will that even his closest friends rarely saw. No one could intrude too deeply upon Will's emotional interior. A dear old friend, Homer Croy, said that beneath the surface, Will was "vastly reserved; there was a wall that no one went beyond; and there were dark chambers and hidden recesses that he opened to no one." Another friend, actor Spencer Tracy, said he was "at the same time, one of the best-known, and one of the least-known, men in the world. By inclination, he is a grand mixer; by instinct, he is as retiring as a hermit." Whenever Will talked about someone else he was witty and brilliant. But when he was asked to talk about himself he was "incurably, painfully shy, ill at ease, embarrassed, eager to escape."[6] Although humor was Will's stock and trade, it was also his refuge. Most likely, the only person with a truly deep understanding of him was his wife.

But times were different back then. Public figures were more guarded about their private lives than they are now. The commonly held attitude was that certain things were just none of the public's business. Celebrities didn't give interviews in which they talked about their deepest fears, how they felt about their parents, or the status of their sex lives. It just wasn't done. In Will's day, it was permissible for a public figure to keep a part of himself for himself.

ROPES AND RESPONSIBILITY

In November of 1996, I did a performance at the Rialto Theater in Loveland, Colorado. After the show, a young man came up to me in the lobby and told me he had always wanted to learn rope tricks. He practically begged me to show him how to do a simple trick or two. I said, "Sure, come on backstage. While I'm packing up I'll show you a few things." As I gave him the basic instructions to a flat spin, he was so intent on what he was doing that his tongue was sticking out the side of his mouth. I said, "Go ahead and frustrate yourself with that for a while. After I get packed up,

I'll show you another one." I turned to the packing job at hand. In a few moments I heard him shout, "Hey! I think I'm getting the hang of this!" When I looked around, I could have been looking at Will Rogers himself. My student was jumping up, over, and through the rope; spinning butterflies, juggles, and ocean waves. I fell to my knees, I was laughing so hard.

This gentleman was Freddie Carlson, nephew of a renowned roper, Lefty Carlson. His uncle had taught him well. Not only was he skilled in the art of roping, but he also had a cowboy's eye for a good practical joke. Freddie's credentials were excellent. When a local troop performed the Broadway hit, *The Will Rogers Follies,* in Boulder, Colorado, he did the amazing roping demonstration that opens the second act. Not being one to miss an opportunity, I said, "Show me how to do some of those." Freddie said, "I'll do better than that. I'll make you up an instructional video and I'll mail it to you in a month or so." I gave him my card and thought that I would never hear from him again. But a cowboy is good for his word. The video arrived as promised. In it Freddie showed me all the keys to the major tricks and set me to practicing in earnest. He improved my show and gave me a good story for my book.

The professional responsibility of performers is to be always improving their skills, whether singing, acting, roping, or comedy. This matter of shooting off your mouth in public is a very serious business. It will either get you shot or make you a good living. Ironically, to be successful at it you cannot take yourself too seriously. You must balance a need for self-discipline with a natural sense of freedom and playfulness. In looking for a mentor in this regard, I fell across a great one in Will Rogers. The way he approached his roping is a good example. On the one hand, the rope was a kind of security blanket that provided him an escape from the pressures of an active life. But at the same time it was a toy — the whole thing was fun. Similar to the way Michael Jordan sinks a fade-away jump shot, Will made his rope tricks appear effortless. Although he was a natural, that does not mean that being the best was easy. Will's casual execution of his most difficult tricks belied the years of conscientious practice that went into mastering them. He was disciplined, but more importantly, when it came time to play, Rogers, like Jordan, loved the game.

Will writing his column in his car

He approached his journalism in the same spirit. He did the hard work that was required. But, after reading countless newspapers, meeting people of all walks of life, and traveling to where the action was, Will would sit down to his "old Carona" and play. He wrote the same way he talked.

His spelling and grammar were atrocious and he knew it. But he was having a good time and his readers were too. He said, "*When I first started out to write and misspelled a few words, people said I was plain ignorant. But when I got all the words wrong, they declared I was a humorist.*"[7]

Will was often asked by college students how one might get into the line of being a humorist. On one particular occasion, a student provided him with a questionnaire, which he used as the basis for an article printed in *American Magazine* in 1929. Although all of the student's questions were in earnest, Will didn't take any of them seriously. He acted as if the whole thing were a joke—and after he got through with it, it was. But if the student was able to read between the lines, he probably learned a lot.

SO YOU WANT TO BE A HUMORIST

"'Is the field of humor crowded?'

"Only when Congress is in session.

"'What talent is necessary? Must one be born with a funnybone in his head?'

"'Its not a talent, its an affliction. If a funnybone is nessasary I would say that in the head is the place to have it. That's the least used of a humorists equipment.

"'What field of Humor offers the best field now and which is most liable to develop?'

"Well, I think the 'Nut' or 'Cuckoo' field is the best bet now, and from what I see of modern America, I think 'Nuttier Still' or 'Super Cuckoo' will be more apt to develop.

"'In training what should one aim for?'

"Aim for Mark Twain, even if you land with Mutt and Jeff.

"'Whats the best way to start being a Humorist?'

"Recovery from a Mule kick is one that's used a lot. Being dropped head downward on a pavement in youth, has been responsible for a lot. And discharge from an Asylum for mental cases is almost sure fire.

"'How should one practice for it after starting it?'

"By reading Editorials in Tabloid Magazines and three pages of the Congressional Record before retiring every night.

"'Should one jot down ideas?'

"No! There will be so few that you can remember them.

"'Should one read other Humorists?'

"If you are Humorist, there is no other Humorist.

"'Is it profitable to read other Humorists?'

"Profitable but terribly discouraging.

"'Do you think it does any good to play the Fool and wit at social gatherings?'

"Not if they will feed you without it. But if you feel that you need the practice and just cant remain normal any longer, why go ahead. Everybody will perhaps want to kill you, and may. As for Social gatherings, I never knew of a Humorist getting into one if it had any social standing.

"'Does College training add to your chances?'

"Yes, nothing enhances a mans humor more than College. Colleges and Ford cars have been indespensible to humor.

"'Should one specialize in any particular subject?'

"Everything but English.

"'What College would you suggest in preperation for a Humorous career?'

"Harvard, if its present football continues.

"'Must one have a heterogenous background of experience?'

"You got me with that hetegenerous. But I will say 'Yes' to that question and take a chance. I want to answer these 100%.

"'Whats the best place to study human nature?'

"At the source.

"'Does a budding Humorist have to wait till he has acquired a philosophy?'

"No, just a 'Carona' typewriter is all.

"'What is the precedure in submitting jokes or skits to Papers or Magazines?'

"A return envelope stamped.

"'How do you get into Syndicate work?'

"Lose all other jobs on a newspaper, or knock 50 home runs, or work 12 years with the Follies, and dodge all Literacy tests.

"'Do you think cartooning has a future?'

"I certainly do. Its never had a boom, just a steady growth. The more we raise that cant read the more look at Pictures.

"'What Magazine would you send your first stories too?'

"The nearest one.

"'Is there such a thing as running stale or getting out of material?'

"I have heard of that happening, but in very rare cases. Every article seems better than the preceeding one, and continues so right up to the execution.

"'This thing you do around the Country where you do a whole evenings entertainment yourself, just what is it?'

"Son, I couldn't tell you. With the old-timers they called it a Lecture. With Politicians they call it a 'Message.' But with me its just a Graft."[8]

RADIO

People who lived through the early 1930s will tell you that if there was anything Will was noted for on the radio, it was his alarm clock. This alarm clock would go off to signal when his time was up. He was so accustomed to working on stage, where he could ramble on about anything the audience was going with, that in his first few ventures into radio he found he was going too long. This was upsetting the sponsors who wanted to air their commercials in a timely manner. Therefore, Will arranged it so that when the alarm clock rang, he would have just enough time to quickly wrap up and say good night. Everyone at home and in the studio audience sat waiting for this thing to go off. It became his radio signature. The first time he brought out the old alarm clock, Will explained, *"The hardest thing over this radio is to get me stopped. So tonight I got me a clock here... When that alarm goes off, I am going to stop, that is all there is to it. I don't care whether I am in the middle of reciting Gunga Din or the Declaration of Independence, I am going to stop right when that rings."*[9]

By 1934, Will was so well known for his self-effacing style that he could pretend to be bragging on himself and everybody knew it was a joke. NBC had been getting a lot of letters from radio listeners regarding studio audiences. About half of them wanted an audience on hand while the other half didn't. Those who didn't want studio audiences figured they were smart enough to know whether something was funny or not without having an audience there to cue them when to laugh. This was long before canned laughter had been invented and people didn't know any better. Will used his own unique brand of tongue-in-cheek braggadocio when responding to this situation. You will notice, he almost said the name of the competing network in this little piece but it didn't seem to bother him much.

COMEDIANS AND THEIR AUDIENCES

"Now the question arises: Is it better to broadcast with or without an audience? Of course, I'm speaking now from the comedian's angle, not the singer or the band's or a public speaker or anything, but the comedian's.

"From the comedian's standpoint, we like the audience. It helps us, you know, and gives us a little encouragement, and Lord knows, we need it. You see, any comedian has dozens of tricks and mannerisms and facial antics that we can get a laugh on, from an audience that can see 'em, but it's naturally lost to you. We was maybe turning a

somersault, or wiggling our ears, or thumbing our nose, or putting our big toe in our mouth, or doing some other marvelously clever trick which we use in a pinch.

Will Rogers and his radio audience

"And then, too, most comedians are...well, they're...they're just funny to look at. They have some odd defect of the face or are just plain homely. Unfortunately, I'm about the only one that's not. Penner or Wynn, Pearl, Benny, and Cantor, in fact any of them that you can mention...well, you have to laugh when you just look at 'em. They're just odd looking, you know. While with me you would say. 'Who is that distinguished looking man walking toward the microphone?' While they command immediate laughter by simply doing nothing, I command a kind of a hushed attention, rather an

awe, you know. Immediately you say, 'There's a man with a message.' While their's is an infectious laugh or smile, mine is of learning, of culture, of quiet dignity – you would say, 'And there is a brain Trust.'

"Now here's another secret about the studio audience: It's people that particularly like you. You know what I mean. It's our audience, and sometimes they'll be quite a few in there who are not our own kinfolk.

"But you all argue it out, and then you let me know. See? Wait a minute. Don't let me know. Don't send me any letters. But you write to these folks that's putting' on this racket.

"It's the Gulf Oil Company, and...I guess it's in care of the National or is this the Colum...? No, no. This is the National. Here's an NBC right in front of me. NBC...No Body Cares...and those are mighty good letters. Nothin' anybody says over the radio today is remembered tomorrow, and it's just as well. No Body Cares. In fact, whatever you say tonight, you can come back on tomorrow night and deny it, in case anybody does remember it, but they don't. But it's the greatest thing in the world, and it's the greatest invention of our lifetime. The radio is the only thing ever invented that didn't knock anybody out of any work.

"Now remember, write to the Gulf Oil Company and let us know, you know, whether you want to hear a lot of laughs and applause or anything you want. You're the boss. Any way you want your radio and all. I hope you all have a fine summer, and I'm going to see you next... [Alarm clock rings] *Oh, here...wait a minute. I wasn't through here yet. I'm going to see you next fall when I get back with a lot of news. Good-bye and good luck."*[10]

MOVIES

Will was singularly unimpressed with his status in the motion picture industry. Although he became the top box office draw of his day and starred in twenty-one smash hit talkies, he thought of movies mainly as entertainment and of himself as a craftsman more than an artist. Privately, he was very serious about making good movies, but publicly he made light of their importance. In discussing the status of actors in general, he said, *"An actor is a fellow that just has a little more monkey in him than a fellow that can't act."*[11] When asked about his personal role in the history of motion pictures, he was inclined to make it into a joke, much the same way he played down his other accomplishments.

WILL'S HISTORY IN PICTURES

"I was in Pictures in Hollywood away back when some of these big stars now were just learning to get married. You see Pictures have to undergo a poor or 'mediocre' stage before they can get to be big. Well, that is the stage that I assisted the great Film Industry through. The minute they commenced to getting better, why my mission had been fulfilled. In other words, I am what you would call a Pioneer. I am all right in anything while it's in its crude state, but the minute it gets to having any class, why I am sunk.[12]

"Now in the old days just looks alone got me by. The Lord was good to me in the matter of handing out a sort of a half breed Adonis profile (well it was a little more than a profile that you had to get). Straight on I didn't look so good, and even sideways I wasn't too terrific, but a cross between a back and a three quarter view, brother I was hot. The way my ear (on one side) stood out

from my head, was just bordering on perfect.

"That rear view gave you just the shot needed. That ear didn't just stick out, it kinder protruded just gently. In those old silent day pictures that back right ear was a by word from Coast to Coast.

"You see all screen stars have what you call their better angles. These women have just certain cameramen to shoot them, they know which way to turn 'em, and how to throw light on 'em. Well, they don't pay much attention to lighting with me, the more lights go out during a scene, the better.[13]

"I hold only two distinctions in the movie business: ugliest fellow in 'em and I still have the same wife I started out with."[14]

There has been a lot of controversy lately about "cleaning up" Hollywood. Politicians have seized on this issue. It allows them to avoid dealing with the really hard stuff like health care, campaign finance reform, and the national debt. But they do have a point. Many of us are legitimately concerned about the effect the media is having on our kids these days. So, naturally, the "free speech versus censorship" argument has become one of our hot-button issues. This is nothing new. Efforts at censorship have been around for a long time. In Will's day, there were countless women's organizations, church groups, and newspaper editorialists who saw themselves as the guardians of official morality. Hollywood was so scandal-ridden in the 1920s that the studios, on their own initiative, appointed Will Hays as a watchdog over their industry. Throughout the silent movie era and on into talkies, he and the studios saw to it that movies, and the private lives of the actors in them, were tightly and legally controlled. Movies were censored at a level the majority of us would not tolerate today.

Because of that, looking back, we must admit that some of the old movies were hokum by today's standards. The great ones among them have survived and rightly so. But because the cream of the crop are still with us, I often hear, "In the good old days the music and the movies were so much better." In truth, the "good old days" were rife with lousy music and dreary movies. But time has a way of preserving the best of any given period. What we now consider classic music, art, and literature had to coexist with a lot of mediocre junk. But after time has done its magic, we look back and think that all the music was Duke Ellington and all the movies were *Casablanca.*

In real life, Hollywood, just like the fast food industry, is a market-driven business. When the fast food folks put healthy food on their menus, the message came back loud and clear, "We don't want this stuff! Give us food that drips down our chins!" What people want to eat is their own business, and sometimes nothing short of a double bacon cheeseburger will do. But when people throughout the country point to Will Rogers and ask me, "Why can't we have that kind of clean wholesome entertainment today?," they are usually somewhat surprised when I answer, "We do." Of course, it doesn't take the exact form it did in Will's day since it is a product of our time, not his. But there is a bounty of wholesome entertainment out there. There are family stories, lovable pigs who win Oscar nominations, wonderful documentaries, fantasies, dramas, clean comedies — you name it! There are also wonderful pictures for those of us who enjoy themes a little more mature than animated features. The frustration lies in how many bad movies make money while smaller labors of love die for lack of an audience. And whose fault is that?

I doubt Will would have a solution for the "free speech versus censorship" argument we are having today. But given Hollywood's eye toward the marketplace, perhaps he would suggest that the only way to get the kinds of movies made that you want to see is to make a market for them. See if the following doesn't bear me out.

WHAT'S THE MATTER WITH THE MOVIES?

"I can't write about the movies for I don't know anything about them, and I don't think anybody else knows anything about them either. It's the only business in the world that nobody knows anything about. Being in them don't give any more of an inkling about them than being out of them.

"They, just a few months ago in New York, had a convention to discuss ways and means of regulating them and fixing a few of the things that they thought was worrying the industry. Well, it didn't get anywhere for nobody knew what was worrying the industry. Everybody knew what was worrying him personally, but there was no two things that was worrying the same person.

"The exhibitor said he wanted better pictures for less money.

"The producer said he wanted better stories and better directors and better actors for less money.

"The actor said: 'You are not giving me a fair share of what I draw at the box office.'

"Will Hays said: 'They got to be cleaner.'

"The exhibitor says: 'If you get them too clean nobody is interested in them.'

"The novelist says: 'What's the use of selling them a story, they don't make the story they buy.'

"The Scenario Staff says: 'It reads good but it won't

photograph.'

"The exchange salesmen say: 'The exhibitors are a dumb lot, they don't know what their audiences want.'

"The exhibitors say: 'We may be dumb, but we know how to count up. Give us pictures where there is something to count up.'

"The so-called intellectual keeps saying: 'Why don't they give us something worthwhile in the movies that we can think about.'

"The regular movie fan says: 'Give us something to see, never mind think about. If we wanted to think we wouldn't come in here.'

"The old married folks say: 'Give us something besides all this love sick junk, and the fadeout behind a willow tree.'

"The young folks that pay the rent on these temples of uplift say: 'Give us some love and romance; what do we care about these pictures with a lot of folks trying to show what they do in life. We will get old soon enough without having to see it now.'

"Wall Street says: 'We want more interest on our money.'

"The producers say: 'Look at the fun you are having by being in this business. Didn't we give you a pass through the studio, what do you want for your money?'

"The actors that aren't working say: 'They don't want actors any more, they only want types.'

"The actors that are working say: 'Thank God they are beginning to realize it's us actors they want and not just somebody that looks like the part.'

Will Rogers and Shirley Temple
on the set of *David Harum*

"Everybody is trying to offer suggestions how to regulate the business and bring it down on a sane basis. They are not going to bring it back on a sane basis. It will keep right on going just like it is now. It was never meant to be sane. It grows and gets bigger in spite of every known handicap.

"You can't get a picture so poor but there won't be an audience growing up somewhere that will like it, and you can't get one so good but what they won't be forty per cent of the people that see it, that won't like it. If it wasn't that way everybody in the world would go to see one picture.

"So they better quit monkeying with the business and

let it alone. It's odd now, but it's odd in all of us movie people's favor.

"The exhibitor that saying he isn't making as much money as he used to, means that he is not making as much as he did last year or the year before, but he doesn't mean that he is not making as much as he was before he got into this business.

"The producer who says things are getting tough in the picture business, you suggest to him to go back into his original line of business and he will punch you in the jaw.

"And the same with the actor, or anyone connected with the business, and the same also with the audience. He starts beefing about poor pictures, when he was never able to go before and get as much amusement for twenty, thirty, forty or fifty cents. He is doing better than he ever was in his life before.

"He used to have to go to the gallery and sit in peanut hulls up to his chin, and come down a long stairs into a dark alley after the show, for more money than he can sit in a wonderful upholstered seat that he didn't even know existed till the movie man built his theater. It's breaking pretty soft for audiences the same as for movie actors and producers and exhibitors.

"Then the highbrow that says pictures are the bunk, let him try and find something that will beat them for twenty-five cents. There is no other branch of amusement in the world that has been brought right to his nearest street corner. They are not bringing opera to your door step, or spoken drama to your neighborhood. You have to go to the city to get them. So don't start yapping about pictures. There is no law in the world that makes you go to them. No sir, you go to them because there is nothing

that has yet been invented that can compare with them for the money.

"These fan magazines are always yowling about, 'What's the matter with the movies?' Try and get any of these editors to go back into their old newspaper work at their old salaries.

"No sir, the movie business is a 'cuckoo' business made by 'cuckoo' people for 'cuckoo' audiences, and as about eighty per cent of the world is 'cuckoo' anyway, they fill a spot that nothing will ever replace unless somebody invents something more 'cuckoo.'

"Everybody is trying to find out what's the matter with them. If they ever do find out they will ruin their own business.

"The movies have only one thing that may ever dent them in any way, and that is when the people in them, or the people going to them, ever start taking them seriously. Call them 'arts and sciences' but do so with your tongue in your cheek. Everything that makes money and gives pleasure is not art. If it was, bootlegging would be the highest form of artistic endeavor.

"So let's everybody connected with them, and everybody that loves to go see them, as we go to our beds at night, pray to our Supreme Being, that he don't allow it to be found out what is the matter with the movies, for if he ever does, we will all be out of a job."[15]

7

WILL'S NEAR-DEATH EXPERIENCE

One of our major concerns today is the state of the health care industry. People can no longer afford to get sick, at least not without a good health insurance policy. For those of us without insurance, a major illness could lead to financial ruin. As our policymakers in Washington engage in endless circular arguments over whose interests should be protected, the average citizen is overwhelmed with the complexity of this issue. The only thing everyone can agree on is that it is all too expensive. As far as we the consumers are concerned, the doctors, lawyers, hospitals, and insurance and pharmaceutical companies are charging too much. But isn't it true that we contribute to the problem? We demand a high level of technology that is very expensive, we are quick to sue hospitals and caregivers if everything doesn't go perfectly, and our expectations, in light of how we take care of ourselves, are very high.

This was not true in Will's day. In Indian Territory, home remedies were the most common forms of treatment. If a doctor was called in, his payment might be a crate of chickens or some other type of barter. These were the days before immunization and penicillin. Broken limbs were one thing – infectious diseases another. Since medicine was a very inexact science, luck played a large role in the cure. So naturally, accountability was minimal. If the doctor failed to save you, he simply told your relatives, "I'm sorry. I did the best I could." They said, "Thanks for trying, Doctor." End of story.

Finding something Will had to say about medicine that would relate to some of what we are feeling today was not an easy task. Frankly, when Will was healthy, he had very little to say about doctors. But fortunately for me (and not so fortunately for him) Will suffered an illness that put him up close and personal with the medical profession. An attack of gallstones, during the summer of 1927 came very close to killing him. Few people outside the doctors and Betty understood just how serious the attack was. But it provided so much material for Will that he created an entire book around the experience, called, *Ether and Me, or 'Just Relax.'* In it he poked good-natured fun at doctors, the insurance industry, and himself.

The following tale, condensed from that book, touches on the universal things that Will had to say on the subject. It plays well to people in the medical profession because, although he made fun of them, Will obviously had great respect for the "machete wielders" who had saved his life – and that respect was well deserved. But Will shared a naivete of his times that promoted an image of doctors as infallible. To many doctors' delight and to a small minority's chagrin, they carry less of that burden today.

FROM
ETHER AND ME

"Now I'm gonna tell you a story about a suffering Actor. Oftentimes you have been made to suffer by Actors. So you will be tickled to death to hear about an Actor who suffers.

"This story opens on the bank of the Verdigris River

in the good old Indian Territory. The plot of the story is a pain in the stomach. The stomach was located amidships of a youth who was prowling up, down, in and across said Verdigris River.

"As I think back on it, we were a primitive people in those days. There were only a mighty few known diseases. Gunshot wounds, broken legs, toothache, fits, and anything that hurt you from the lower end of your neck on down as far as your hips was known as a bellyache. Gallstones would have struck us as something that the old-time Gauls would heave at the Philistines or maybe get up on Mount Mussolini and roll them down on 'em.

"Well, in those days, there was no such thing as indigestion, on account of everybody worked.

"I don't remember when I first had it, but regardless, the old plot of the piece, the stomach ache, she would play a return date on me about every couple of years.

"It hadn't shown up in years, until one spring, on my tour of national annoyances, I hit a town called Bluefield, West Virginia. I hadn't been there long when the old plot showed up. Now ordinarily when a pain hits you in the stomach in Bluefield, West Virginia, you would take it for gunshot wounds. But the old town has quieted down now and the sharpshooters have all joined the Kiwanis and Rotary Clubs. So I knew it wasn't wounds. Also, the pain struck me before the nightly lecture and I knew that no one would shoot me before the lecture, unless by chance he had heard it over in another town.

"Well, the next time it hit me was just a few weeks later, out at my old ranch on the Verdigris River. You see, now the plot is slowly thickening. Instead of quitting me after a few hours, as it generally had, it kept hanging on. So, my wife called in Doctor White, a famous physician.

He would lay his hand on my stomach and thump the back part of his own hand with his other one.

"'What part of your stomach hurts?' he'd ask me.

"'Practically all of it, Doc.' I says.

"'How about there?' He says, thumping and feeling around where I had always been led to believe the appendix is.

"I says 'There's where you are wrong, Doc; that's the only part that don't hurt.'

"He says, 'Are you sure there's no pain there?'

"'I'm absolutely sure, Doctor.' I says.

"Well, that seemed to kind of lick him. An appendicitis operation within his grasp, and here it was slipping through his hands. He looked kind of discouraged. He began to take soundings around the upper end of the stomach. When I told him that was where the pain was worse, his face began to brighten up.

"Then he turned and exclaimed with a practiced and well-subdued enthusiasm, 'It's the Gall Bladder…just what I was afraid of.'

"Then he casually inquired if I had had a good season. I told him that outside of Waxahachie, Texas,…Hershey, Pennsylvania,…Concord, New Hampshire, and Newton, Kansas, I had got by in paying quantities.

"He then says, 'We operate.' My wife says, 'Operate?' And as soon as I came to enough I says, 'Operate?'

"My wife says, 'Is there no easier way out?'

"Then I showed that the pain had not entirely dulled my intellect. I says, 'Yes, is there no cheaper way out?'

"'No,' he says. 'You will always be bothered. The best way is to have them taken out. Where's the phone?'

"Well, he phoned for what seemed like a friend, but who afterwards turned out to be an accomplice. These

doctors nowadays run in pairs and bunches, you know.

"This is a day of specializing, especially with the doctors. Say, for instance, there is something the matter with your right eye. You go to a doctor and he tells you, 'I am sorry, but I am a left-eye doctor; I make a specialty of left eyes.' Take the throat business for instance. A doctor that doctors on the upper part of your throat, he doesn't even know where the lower part goes to.

"The old fashioned doctor didn't pick out a big toe or a left ear to make a life's living on. He picked the whole human frame. No matter what end of you was wrong, he had to try to cure you single-handed. Personally, I have always felt that the best doctor in the world is the Veterinarian. He can't ask his patients what is the matter...he's got to just know.

"Well, after a while I heard a big expensive car coming up our driveway hill. It made it in high gear without a shift. This fellow came right on upstairs, and they met.

"There was a kind of knowing look between them, as good as to say, 'I think we can get him.' Dr. White's accomplice was Dr. Clarence Moore, the operating end of the firm. He is the most famous machete wielder on the Western Coast.

"The first doctor said, 'What do you think?' The second one says, 'I think Gallstones.'

"The first one says, 'That's what I said.'

"I says, 'I'm glad you boys are guessing together.'

"'What do you advise?' the first doctor asked.

"'I advise an operation,' said the second.

"'That's what I advised,' said the first.

"Imagine asking a surgeon what he advises! It would be like asking Coolidge, 'Do you advise economy?'

"My wife said, 'When?' The whole thing seemed to

have gone out of my hands. I was just laying there marked Exhibit A.

"Number One rushed to the phone again and called up. I was relieved to hear that it was only the hospital he was calling. The only other feller I could think of was the Undertaker. He was asking for a nice room. I heard him say, 'Yes, we'll be there in the morning.'

"My wife asks him, 'Doctor, is there any danger in this operation?'

"And you know, they replied, together in unison; 'Why, there is just about a half of one per cent,' as though they had rehearsed it or something.

"They were reaching for their hats and all smiling, and you would have thought we had all made a date to have some fun."

Will Rogers from *Dr. Bull*

Before letting Will go off to the hospital, you should know that ether was not Will's first experience with gas and his gallbladder attack was not his first brush with death. Will got gassed the first time accidentally. In his early cowboy days, he and a partner were entrusted with the management of a trainload of cattle to be delivered in California. After the delivery, the two boys visited San Francisco, where they stayed in a modern hotel that used gas lighting. Upon retiring for the night, the partner, being used to oil lamps, blew out the flame. The gas seeped into the room, and the next morning the two cowboys were found unconscious. Emergency room doctors came very close to losing them both. After returning home, Will went into a long period of recuperation, taking several weeks to get the gas out of his system.

As Will's story unfolds, you will find him continuing to make fun of his latent cowardly nature. Perhaps it had as much to do with the ether as it did with going under the knife. Will made fun. But in reality, he probably wasn't looking forward to being gassed again.

"Well, the household was up bright and early next morning to get old Dad off to the hospital.

"Oh, yes, I like to forgot to tell you that during this time I was turning yellow. One of the symptoms of the Gall is that it produces jaundice.

"Well, the doctors were both remarking. 'Very yellow…uh huh…he is getting yellower.' Ha…ha! They didn't know it, but I wanted to tell them that that yellow was from the heart and not from the liver and gall bladder.

"The next morning, in filed this battalion of doctors…and Betty was with them. They discussed it all

between themselves. I, the defendant, wasn't put on the stand at all. Finally they filed out. I wanted to get a chance to instruct the jury, but nothing doing. The clinic was over.

"Then there was a knock on the door and the jury came in. It stood all four for operation. They all went out, but forgot to shut the door, and I heard my two bidding the other two good-by, thanking them...you know...saying, 'We'll do as much for you sometime, boys.'

"Oh, they were tickled to death. They being doctor golfers, you would have thought they had broken a hundred and ten.

"Well, I didn't have any kind of a shirt or nightgown on. I had a sheet kind of draped over me. All I needed was my hands crossed. Then they tied a white thing around my head. Then all I needed was a Klan card.

"The doctor had a thing over his mouth so he wouldn't catch the same disease I had.

"I was on the wagon and all ready. Then we got the signal that we were next. I bid good-by to my Betty and the parade started down the hall to the elevator. We passed another wagon with an old boy on it that had just come down. I heard him cussing, and I thought: 'He's all right, and even if he passes out, he will have the satisfaction of telling them what he thought of them before he left.'

"As I am a-rolling to the operating room with a retinue of nurses and doctors as outriders, I thought I ought to pull some kind of a gag when I got in there that would get a laugh. There was a kind of a little balcony up above the operating room floor where people with a well developed sense of humor could sit and see other people cut up. It must be loads of fun. But there wasn't a soul in

there for my operation. I felt kind of disappointed.

"I thought, 'Well, here I am maybe playing my last act, and it to an empty house.'

"One fellow had a kind of a hose with a big nozzle on the end of it. Well, I had by this time thought of my joke and was all ready to pull it and set the whole place in a good natured uproar. I just opened my mouth to utter my comical wheeze when this old hose boy just gently slipped that nozzle right over my mouth and nose both. Well, I started to reach up and snatch it off, and a couple of men who had enlisted as interns, but who in reality were wrestlers on vacation, had me by each hand. I certainly was sore. Here I had this last aspiring wise crack and it had been snuffed out before I could give vent to it. And what made it so bad, I can't think to this day what it was.

"You see the first thing they bump you off with is gas. Then they give you the ether...with the ether comes dream time.

"First the birds started singing, but they only sang a minute, when we had a shipwreck and everybody on the boat was going down, and it looked like they were trying to push me under.

"Then a farmer started running and hollering for relief, when somebody shot him to put him out of his mortgages. Then I was in a bus trying to make a grade crossing.

"Well, the train was right on us when the Chinese started shelling the town and saying, 'We are Missionaries come to America, and you will have to worship Buddha and go to the Mission schools and learn Chinese.' Then the Nicaraguans started dropping airplane bombs on us. We had nothing to do but let them drop. They said, 'They wanted to protect the United States, as they wanted to put

a canal through here some time.'

"Then I was rehearsing with the Follies. Coolidge and I were working together. Then the water kept rising till it got up around the bed and there were women and children and horses and mules and levees and cotton gins and airplanes and boats.

"Then another crevasse broke and we were drowning...and then...I heard the nurse on one side and my wife on the other both saying, 'Lay perfectly still, you're all right. You are fine now. Just relax.'

"How was I going to do anything else? Wasn't every bone in my body broke?

"'You'll be all right.'...you know...'Just relax and go back to sleep. Yes dear, it's all over and you are fine.'

"'What's fine? I don't see anything fine. Didn't the airship burn up and me right in it?'

"She says, 'It's the ether.'

"'No, it's not the ether' I says. 'I know what I'm doing...I'm dying, and you-all are just standing there while I do it.'

"Finally this ether got to leaving me and I sort of remembered what the operation had been for.

"Well, as things proceeded, I would keep seeing the doctors and nurses coming in and looking down on the floor at the side of my bed. I thought at first it was a dog under the bed. But they would frown and look worried and then move away.

"It seems all this worry was from the fact that I wasn't draining. I didn't have sense enough to know it, but I was in pretty bad shape. Well, the doctors slept right there at the hospital. They were trying everything from glucose to Murphy's Drip. Things were looking bad for Claremore, Oklahoma's favorite lightheaded comedian.

If things didn't show up pretty soon, it looked like I had annoyed my last President.

"But finally it showed up. Doctor Moore got one look and was so tickled that I believe if I had paid my bill then I would have gotten fifty per cent off.

"He then sits down and takes a card out of his pocket and draws a blue print of the whole thing for me. Well, he explained it so easy that I was sorry I hadn't taken up doctoring, for it looked mighty simple.

"Now the Gall goes into this little pocket and remains until needed...that is, until you get sore at somebody and want to use it up on them, that's why it is...that good natured people are the ones that have the Gall operations; they never get a chance to use it up on anybody.

"Another thing I learned is that the complaint is more common by far among women than it is among men. Well, that fact didn't please me so much, as I was just bordering on the effeminate as it was.

"I also learned that it was more prevalent among Jewish people; that's what I get for going to those Kosher restaurants with Eddie Cantor.

"Now, as I have so thoroughly and comprehensively explained this, the question now is, 'What causes the stones to form?' Well, there are various reasons. Republicans staying in power too long will increase the epidemic; seeing the same ending to Moving Pictures all the time is a prime cause.

"But while laying in the hospital recuperating I just accidentally stumbled on what I really think caused the operation. For years I had carried a very big...that is, big for my circumstances...Accident and Sickness Disability Insurance. Well, I would notice that when it would come time to pay the premiums it seemed like a bad investment.

"It was getting terribly discouraging to keep paying year after year and not being able to get sick. Here I was betting a lot of insurance companies that I would get sick and they were betting me that I wouldn't. Now if you think you are not a sucker in a case like that, all you have to do is to look at the financial standing of the company in comparison to the financial standing of the people who bet on the other side.

"Why, these insurance companies have the highest priced doctors to look you over. And then, if you look like nothing but lightening can kill you, why, the doctor sends in a report to the company to go ahead and bet you that you won't get sick. But if you look the least bit like you are going to get sick, they won't bet you. Any time they approve of you, that should show you right there that there is nothing going to happen to you. But you, like a fool, go ahead and bet them in the face of all this professional knowledge that you know more than they do.

"Well here's the deal. I had this Accident and Disability Insurance because I thought it was important.

"I had argued with my wife, saying, 'Well, I may get sick.'

Well, she kinda leaned the other way saying, 'Yes, you might get sick, but you never do.'

"So last Summer when paying time came, my insurance man advised her to reduce the policies. Well, I didn't know the thing had been cut down.

"One day I was a-laying in the hospital and I just happened to have the only bright thought that had come to me in weeks. So when my wife called, I broke the good news to her.

"I says, 'If we can get a bona-fide doctor to say that I have been sick and couldn't spin a rope and talk about

Coolidge, we are in for some disability.' Well, I noticed the wife didn't seem so boisterous about this idea. Then the truth did slowly come out; she told me the sad story of the cutting down of the insurance. It read like a sentence to me. She said my physical condition had misled them.

"So if you want to stay well, just bet a lot of rich companies that you will get sick. Of course I got this consolation: If I had had the bigger policy, why, it would have had some clause in there where I got sick on the wrong day or had the wrong disease or that policy didn't cover rock quarries. Something like that. There would have been an alibi in it somewhere, for those four pages of clauses in a policy are not put in there just to make it longer. So I guess everything happened for the best. After all, it's not the operation that's bad; it's the caster oil afterward, I suppose.

"And you know, we kid about our Doctors and we hate to pay 'em after it's all over and we've quit hurting. But I expect a lot of us have got 'em to thank for being here.[1]

"Besides, people couldn't have been nicer to me if I had died."[2]

8

ALL THAT DRINKIN' AND GAMBLIN'

In January of 1919, the Eighteenth Amendment to the Constitution was ratified, establishing Prohibition. Later that same year, Will compiled many of his Ziegfeld Follies comments on the subject into a short book called *The Cowboy Philosopher on Prohibition.* From the beginning, Will seemed to think this effort to legislate morality was an exercise in futility. The following condensation of his comments suggests that Will thought Prohibition was extreme and its proponents, the "drys," were prone to hysteria.

FROM *THE COWBOY PHILOSOPHER ON PROHIBITION*

"Now, before I start in, I want it distinctly understood I don't knock Prohibition through any personal grudge as I do not drink myself. But I do love to play to an audience who have had a few nips, just enough so they can see the joke and still sober enough to applaud it.

"But, you know, the Prohibitionists just seem to be sore on the World. First off, they claim it was necessary to put it through as a war measure. Well, how about this? France fought quite a bit in the war and trained on Wine. England did her part on Scotch and Polly and Ale. Canadian Club furnished its Quota from Canada. Italy

Chiantied over the Alps into Austria. Womens clothes and Scotch Whiskey didn't keep the Highlanders back much. Guinnesses Stout kept the Irish fighting as usual. The American Troops didn't retreat any further than you can run your hand in a Paper Bag and they had been used to old Crow and Kentucky Bourbon. Russia was doing fine till some nut took their Vodka away from them and they went back to look for it and nobody has ever heard of them since. Germany the Country with the smallest percentage of Alcohol in their National drink (which is beer) and Turkey who are totally prohibition – why they lose the war.

"Now a Prohibitionist is a man or woman, who is so self satisfied with himself that he presents himself with a Medal, called the 'CROIX DE PERFECT HE.' He gives himself this Medal because he is now going to start to meddle in everybodys business but his own.

"Look at these Towns and people after Prohibition has hit them. Everybody looks like they had just had a puncture and no extra tire. They look like they had just heard the Kaiser had invaded Belgium again.

"Of course on the other hand it has introduced a lot of new methods especially in regard to getting it in to dry territory. They put it in extra tires and even in the ones they were running on. One day a fellow had a couple of blow outs on the way into Oklahoma and lost all the profits.

"But, you know, the minute they get Prohibition they will hop on to something else…it will be Cigarettes or something. I see where they propose to stop Cigarettes first and then profanity. They are going to have a tough time with that profanity, cause as long as there is a prohibitionist living there will be profanity. !ZR_Z??ZIZ,!R_R_R_Z!!!*

"Just look. Maine and Kansas were the first Prohibition states, now look at them. Maine was noted for two things, one was drinking awful whiskey and the other was shooting another hunter. The principal industry of Kansas was bootlegging. The only way you could tell a Citizen from a Bootlegger in Kansas was the bootlegger would be sober. Billy Sunday said when we get prohibition that there wont be any more jails. Kansas and Maine have more in them than out.

"Folks, you don't have to go any farther than our best ancient writers to prove that prohibition was unnecessary, look at old OMAR KHAYHAM, 'The Pickled Philosopher of Persia.' Do you think Billy Sundays SLANG will live as long as Omars Philosophy has? He says he, 'divorced old barren reason and took the daughter of the Vine to spouse.' Have you ever heard a dry say anything that smart?"[1]

Later, in 1927, Will hadn't changed his views much, and he was getting pretty tired of the hypocrisy of it all. *"If you think this Country ain't dry, you just watch 'em vote; and if you think this country ain't wet, you just watch 'em drink. You see, when they vote, it's counted; but when they drink, it ain't."*[2]

Will had gotten a tremendous amount of comedic mileage out of Prohibition over the years. But by the time of his radio broadcast in June of 1930, it was starting to become old. The discussion had atrophied, like so many of our hot-button issues today. Arguments were polarized and everybody was preaching to the choir. After eleven years of Prohibition, Will didn't see much hope for a change. Therefore, when asked to speak on the subject in 1930, instead of addressing those with extreme views, Will directed his comments to those caught in the middle.

NOAH WAS A "WET"

"I have received more letters in the last few weeks to talk on Prohibition than on any other subject. I haven't said a word about it. I wanted to be original and just let it alone. I have yet to hear anybody talk on it that wasn't some kind of a fanatic, no matter which side they was on. But of course a fanatic is always the fellow that is on the opposite side.

"But with all the shoutin' and ravin', I will bet you there hasn't been a single soul converted to the other side. They haven't changed a vote. It's one of those things like religion…you have your mind made up and you don't want anybody coming around trying to tell you what to think.

"I have often said that I wish the wets would become so soused they would be speechless and couldn't say anything, and that the drys would become so perfect that the Lord would come down and take them away from here, and that would leave the country to the rest of us who are tired of listening to both of them.

"The real wet is going to drink I don't care what your laws are, and a real dry is going to lecture to him while he is drinking, no matter what your laws about it are. You can't change human nature. But while those two are fighting it out, there will be 500 passing by, tending to their own business, living their own lives, and doing exactly what they think is best for them.

"We are trying to settle something here that has been going on since way back in Bible times. Right in the first book of Genesis, you don't read but just a few pages until Noah was lit up like a pygmy golf course. Here is just how

it started. Right in the start of Genesis it says, 'And Noah became a husbandman and planted a vineyard.' The minute he became a husband he started in raising the ingredients that goes with married life. So you can trace all drink to marriage, see? What we got to prohibit is marriage.

"In the very next verse it says, 'And he drank of the wine and was drunk.' Now you see Noah drank and he didn't drink water. He was a man that knew more about water than practically any man of his time. He was the Water Commissioner of his day. But the Lord is very far-seeing, and everything He does is for the best.

"Through Noah partaking of too much wine and going on this little spree, that is just why the Lord picked on him to pick out these animals to take into the Ark. He was the only man that had even seen all of them. So if Noah hadn't got drunk, today we would be without circuses and menageries.

"Of course, other men since Noah's time have claimed that they have seen animals that Noah didn't put into the Ark, but they were drinking from a different vineyard.

"You know this wine had such ill effects on Noah that he only lived to be 950 years old. That is just 19 years short of Methuselah, who held the longevity record of his and all times.

"Now, another thing, don't get the idea that Prohibition is staying in the Constitution on account of its moral grounds; it is economics. Big business don't care about what your morals are, but they do care about how much work you can turn out in a day's time. If somebody invented an alcoholic stimulant tomorrow whereby everyone taking a swig of it would start right in working hard and keep it up for eight hours, the country would

vote wet in a month.

"Of course, they are drinking some terrible stuff. You know, in the old days you had to be born courageous. But now they bottle courage. You take one dram of this White Mule and you go out and meet a street car head on purposely. Europe is even trying to find out how we make it. They have never experienced the sensation of unconsciousness without an anaesthetic before. After assaying hundreds of bottles, the only thing they found out, that each bottle held in common with the other bottle, was that it all flowed and death was inevitable.

"Now listen here, folks, honest, this is what I want to get over to you tonight, let's not all get excited about it and break friendship with our neighbors and fall out with our brother over this Prohibition. Talking about Prohibition is like whittling used to be, it passes away the time but don't settle anything."[3]

Another scene from *Dr. Bull*

Will seemed relieved when Prohibition was finally repealed in 1933. In a radio broadcast that year, he praised Franklin Delano Roosevelt for taxing liquor. *"Roosevelt says, 'Just give me three words.' He says, 'Let 'em drink.' That's all. He says, 'Let 'em drink.' And he collected $10 million in revenue in the first two weeks, and if he'd had good beer, he'd have paid the national debt by now."*[4]

Whenever you pass a law forbidding or debarring a substance or practice, you create a demand for such things to be met illegally. Today there are calls for prohibition of everything from pornography to abortion, handguns to flag burning. These issues are lightning rods on our political landscape. The arguments are heated, but the vast majority of Americans have settled for something in the middle ground. We don't want a total ban on our freedoms, but we don't want to set a tone of permissiveness either.

There seems to be one exception to this rule: When it comes to gambling, more and more, we are inclined to look the other way. The middle ground on this issue used to be that people were happy to confine their gambling to Las Vegas, Atlantic City, race tracks, bingo, or the stock market. But now, casinos and riverboat gambling are booming all across the country. Almost every state has a lottery, while casinos on Indian reservations make up one of the largest segments of the gaming industry. Will might have found the irony of this humorous. He would have loved to see the Indians get back some of what they lost to the white man by gambling on his treaties.

But, politically speaking, Will might wonder why liberals are not vehemently opposed to this gambling trend. Studies show that gambling is, in effect, a regressive tax levied on those least able to afford it. It takes money from people with low and moderate incomes and puts most of it into the pockets of the wealthy. The rest goes into the coffers of the state. Traditionally, the Left has been opposed to such taxation.

But he might also wonder why conservatives are not protesting against the proliferation of gambling. Lately, their loudest battle cry has been issued in defense of the family. Studies have shown that gambling can be very addictive. It has resulted in financial ruin for many breadwinners, thus wreaking havoc on American families. There is also some evidence to show that gambling establishments harm local economies, because money that might have been spent at the local hardware store to build a new carport or sundeck gets diverted into a slot machine or a crap table.

Why is it that our liberal and conservative politicians are so silent about the down side of legalized gambling? For one thing, many voters see the decision to gamble as a personal choice, and any attempt to limit that choice, prohibition. But even more importantly, widespread gambling represents an easy way for lawmakers to get revenue for government programs without having to face the music for raising taxes. Will knew this. He said,

> *"You know, people don't mind spending their money if they know it's not going for taxes. Monaco has the right idea. Fix a Game where you are going to get it, but the fellow don't know that you're getting it. A fellow can always get over losing money in a game of chance, but he seems so constituted that he can never get over money thrown away to a Government in Taxes. In other words, he will bet you on anything, but he won't pay it to you in Taxes."*[5]

Will tried his hand at serious gambling only once. While traveling the world in his youth, he got into a card game. At the same moment he lost all of his hard-earned money, he lost all of his interest in gambling. After that, he engaged in no speculations of any kind and invested only in land.

During the Roaring Twenties, many were betting in the stock market, buying stocks on margin, extending their credit, and living the high life. Will warned against such extravagances. If he were here today, he might issue the same warning, saying, *"Americans have been getting away pretty soft up to now. Every time we needed anything, why it was growing right under our nose. Every natural resource in the world, we had it. But with them getting less, and debts getting more, there is going to be some work going on in this country some day."*[6]

Investing in the stock market in the 1920s in many ways parallels our driving habits today. Everybody was flying down the road tailgating each other, and everything was fine until somebody hit the brakes. In October of 1929, somebody hit the brakes. The market crashed and the party was over. Investors who were multimillionaires one day were literally penniless the next. Upon losing their fortunes, many on Wall Street committed suicide by jumping from the tall buildings. The catastrophe that followed has been a vivid national memory ever since. But as time moves on, the reality of the Crash and the Great Depression has started to recede into the past. Now only a few of us have a vague recollection of the hardship our parents and grandparents suffered. We have little personal experience from which to imagine what a crash would mean to us today.

At the time of the crash, Will was very busy making talking movies and keeping his column going. Initially he made light of the whole situation. In his Daily Telegram, he had some advice for any would-be investors. He said, *"There is one rule that works in every calamity. Be it pestilence, war or famine, the rich get richer and the poor get poorer. The poor even help arrange it. But it's just like I have been constantly telling you, 'Don't gamble'; take all your savings and buy some good stock, and hold it till it goes up, then sell it. If it don't go up, don't buy it."*[7]

At first, Will, like everyone else, didn't seem to realize the depth of the crisis. He took the position that we had become overindulgent and the collapse of the economy was just "a return to normalcy." He felt that as a nation we had gone too far with our love of comfort and our desire for easy money. Later on, by word and deed, Will showed broad compassion for those who suffered from the Great Depression. He spent much of his time trying to keep up morale. But initially, he saw clear-cut reasons for the crash and he just "called 'em like he saw 'em."

A NATION OF GAMBLERS

"Oh it was a great game while it lasted. All you had to do was to buy and wait till the next morning and just pick up the paper and see how much you made, in print. But all that has changed, and I think it will be good for everything else. For after all everybody just can't live on gambling. Somebody has to do some work.[8]

"Why, we have been just going like a house afire, and we couldn't see any reason why we shouldn't keep right on burning. We didn't see how we could ever run out of fuel. Our tastes were acquired on credit, and we wanted to keep on enjoying 'em on credit. But a guy knocks on the back door during the year 1930 and says, 'Here, pay for the old radio or we will haul down your aerial.' 'Get out of that

bath tub, we got to take it back.' 'Get out of that hoot nanny, you been driving it without payments long enough.'

"Well, that was a sort of a jar. The man talked so nice when he sold it to us, we had no idea he would ever want it back. Why we had kinder got used to all this, and took it as a matter of fact. If you never had a fifty cents cigar why a nickel one is mighty satisfying, but let you get to puffing on a real one for awhile and the old nickel one is going to be mighty nauseating.

"You see in the old days there was mighty few things bought on credit. Your taste had to be in harmony with your income...for it had never been any other way. But now, I don't reckon there has ever been a time in American homes when there was as much junk in 'em as there is today. Most everybody has got more than they used to have, but they haven't got as much as they thought they ought to have.

"But you see, the Lord was wise to the World and he just wanted to show 'em that, after all, he was running things, in spite of the New York Stock Exchange. Well, that was a terrible blow to finance to learn that the Lord not only closed the Market on Sundays, but practically closed it on week days.[9]

"Yea, the Lord just kinder looked us over and says, 'Wait, you folks are going too fast, slow up and look yourself over, a year of silent meditation will do you good. Then when you start again, you will know you got to get it by working and not by speculation.'[10]

"Time was we used to call depression a State of mind, but now it's a state of health, it's moved from the mind to the stomach. But it's really not depression, it's just a return to normalcy. It's just getting back to two bit meals and cotton underwear, and off those $1.50 steaks and

silk Rompers. America has been just muscle bound from holding a steering wheel. The only callus place we got on our body is the bottom of the driving toe. We are getting back to earth and it don't look good to us after being away so long. [11]

"You know, our whole Depression was brought on by gambling… not alone in the stock market but in expanding and borrowing and going in debt, all just to make some money quick. That's because we like to gamble. We really do. We like to take a chance. We take 'em every day in a car rushing to save a minute with nothing to do when we get the minute saved.[12]

"But it is my feeling that betting is a form of unintelligence. So long as we have betting, we will know we have the ignorant with us.[13]

"As for me, I never in my life made a single dollar without having to chew some gum to get it."[14]

9

"BOODGETARY" MATTERS

On the weekend of what would have been Will's 114th birthday (November 4, 1993), I was asked to be the parade marshal for the Will Rogers Days Celebration in Claremore, Oklahoma. It was a tremendous, unexpected honor that I cherish to this day. Not only did I get to meet many of Will's close relatives and numerous Will Rogers fans from all over the country, but I was asked to do a performance at the Will Rogers Memorial Auditorium as part of the weekend's festivities. Needless to say, playing to an audience filled with Will's home town folks and various authorities on Will's life was a scary prospect. How could I ever do justice to their hero and "Oklahoma's Favorite Son"?

Ten minutes before I went on, I called my wife, Debra, back in Chicago, seeking a little comfort for my "mild" case of nerves. True to form, she gave me the words I needed to carry me through. She said, "Honey, just do like you always do. Go out there and dazzle them with your sincerity." In doing just that, I found my audience had not come to judge the performance as much as to share in my enthusiasm for Will and what he stood for. They gave me one of the warmest receptions I have had anywhere. In those hallowed halls I could almost hear Will saying, "*You can roam all over the World, but after all, it's what the people at home think of you that really counts.*"[1]

Among those gathered for the festivities was Jim Rogers and his son, Kem. To hobnob with Will's direct blood line was a rare opportunity, and I relished it. Jim is just as natural a man as you could ever want to meet. As a rancher in Bakersfield, California, he lives the life his father might have lived had he not gone into show business.

Naturally, from the minute I met Jim, I was anxious to start picking his brain about his father. So, with the timing of a green Washington reporter I blurted out, "Gosh Jim! What was it like to be the son of the most admired and respected man in the country?" In much the same way I imagine his father would have done, Jim said, "Lance, a steer doesn't care who your parents are." Spoken like a true cowboy and a true Rogers.

Jim is a good talker – full of stories and good humor. It is fun to listen to his little inside anecdotes about life with his dad. He attended New Mexico Military Institute in Roswell, New Mexico, about the same time my father did. But like his father before him, Jim wasn't cut out for the military life. When Jim washed out of NMMI, Will felt compelled to give his son a little fatherly lecture on the subject, asking him why he didn't do better. Jim replied, "For the same reason you ran away from Kemper." Betty overheard the exchange and just burst out laughing. Will never brought up the subject again.

Hanging around with these fellas is an education. During some down time at the Memorial, we had an old film of Will running, and in it he said the word "boodget." Jim said to Joe Carter (Director of the Memorial), "Did you hear that? He always said that. He never said 'budget.' It was always 'boodget.'" Our "boodgets," both national and personal, were of great concern to Will. While many people think of him as liberal because of his "live and let live" attitude, when it came to government, taxes, and debt, Will was a bit conservative even by today's standards. He never complained about paying his taxes, mind you, even though he paid handsomely. He thought being an honest taxpayer was just a given, saying, *"It's a great country but you can't live in it for nothing."*[2] But he did criticize the inefficiency of government and questioned how the taxes were being used. Will lamented, *"Lord, the money we do spend on government. And it's not a bit better government than we got for one-third the money twenty years ago."*[3]

Kem Rogers, Lance Brown, and Jim Rogers in the Rotunda of the Will Rogers Memorial, Claremore, Oklahoma

Unlike politicians of almost every stripe today, Will was murder on credit, debt, and speculation by individuals, as well as by governments. Today, very few of us line up with his thinking on financial matters. When we hear Will's common sense viewpoint on these "boodgetary matters," we can't help but wonder how we have drifted so far from the frugality of our ancestors. Even so, in the midst of all our extravagance, we have been making a half-hearted effort at reducing wasteful spending, big government, and bureaucracy. The liberal versus conservative debate is over who should suffer the consequences of balancing the budget; the poor in fewer programs or the wealthy in higher taxes?

From what I have gathered in my travels, average Americans don't want the government gutted, they just want it fixed. At first, many of us thought that we did want it gutted. But when we discovered that in the process we ourselves would have to take a hit, we backed off. Ironically, we want more prisons, better schools, cheaper health care, increased social security, more paid holidays, three cars for every family, and at the same time, less traffic, a clean environment, and lower taxes. It's getting to where the poor politician doesn't know what to promise us anymore. We all have our credit cards maxed out but we want the government to live within its means. I'm sure if Will were here today, these contradictions would provide plenty of inspiration. Will was raised during a time when credit was the exception rather than the rule. People bought very little until they had saved the money to pay for it. So, as the country moved into the Roaring Twenties, with its more extravagant life styles, stock market speculation, and purchasing of modern conveniences on credit, Will cast a jaundiced eye on the whole affair.

CREDIT

"I was raised on a Cattle Ranch and I never saw or heard of a Ranchman going broke. Only the ones who had borrowed money. You can't break a man that don't borrow; he may not have anything, but Boy! he can look the World in the face and say, 'I don't owe you Birds a nickel.'[4]

"But today, we don't have to worry about anything. No nation in the history of the world was ever sitting as pretty. If we want anything, all we have to do is go and buy it on credit. So that leaves us without any economic problem whatever, except perhaps some day to have to pay for them.[5]

"Brothers, we are riding mighty, mighty high in this country. Our most annoying problem is, 'Which car will I use today?' or 'Isn't that static frightful?' We are just sitting on top of the world. For every automobile we furnish an accident. For every radio sold we put on two murders. Three robberies to every bathtub installed. Building two golf courses to every church. Our bootleggers have manicures and our farmers have mortgages. Our courts are full, our jails are full, our politicians are full. If we can't house a prisoner, we burn him up.

"Truly, Rome never saw such prosperity. We'll tell the cockeyed world we are going somewhere."[6]

Of course, borrowing, whether you are a consumer or a government, drives you further into debt—and debt means interest. Will was concerned about our national debt when it could be measured in the tens of billions of dollars. It has now ballooned to over five trillion!

DEBT

"I'll tell you, this country is just livin' off a dollar down and a dollar a day. President Coolidge says that we are approaching an era of prosperity. Everybody generally admits that we are better off than we ever were in our lives, yet we owe a national debt of almost 30 billion dollars. We owe more money than any nation in the world and WE ARE LOWERING TAXES! When is the time to pay off a debt if it is not when you are doing well? All Government statistics say that 70 percent of every dollar paid in the way of taxes goes to just the keeping up of Interest and a little dab of amortization of our National Debts. In other words, if we didn't owe anything our taxes would be less than one third what they are today. Now, here is what I can't savvy. Why is it that one of us, in fact all of us, will work and save and stint all our lives...and for what? Why, to leave something to our children. We will break our necks to leave them without a single debt. In fact, we don't die if we can help it till we get out of debt for their sake. Now that is what we will do as individuals. But when it comes to collectively, why it looks like we'll break our necks just trying to see how much we can leave 'em owing.[7]

"You see, we never will get anywhere with our finances till we pass a law saying that every time we appropriate something we got to pass another bill along with it stating where the money is coming from.[8] *Because a debt is just as hard for a government to pay as it is for an individual. No debt ever come due at a good time. Borrowing is the only thing that is handy all the time."*[9]

Finally, after years of unbridled speculation, a market was created that did not reflect the true financial condition of the country. In October of 1929, the balloon burst. The stock market crashed and we entered into an economic depression from which we would not fully recover until after World War II.

Will, and most of the people of his day, had been through fluctuations in the economy before. Hard times would come and go. People managed. But as hardship deepened, it became apparent that the Great Depression was something far beyond the norm. Responding to the suffering of the unemployed and the impoverished, Will spent over half of his time and fortune on relief work. His heart was with the working class when he said,

> *"Here is what George Washington missed by not living to his 199th birthday. He would have seen our great political system of 'equal rights to all and privileges to none' working so smoothly that 7,000,000 are without a chance to earn their living.*

Will doing relief work in England, Arkansas

"He would see 'em handing out rations in peacetime that would have reminded him of Valley Forge. In fact, we have reversed the old system. We all get fat in war times and thin during peace. I bet after seeing us he would sue us for calling him 'Father.'[10]

"What's the matter with this country anyhow? No country ever had more, and no country ever had less. Ten men in our country could buy the whole world and ten million can't buy enough to eat."[11]

In an effort to stimulate the economy and create jobs, government programs were being developed under FDR that funneled tremendous amounts of money into public works projects and bailing out businesses. Will tried to get a handle on just how much money was being spent.

"The President signed another loan bill. This one for only 125 million for land banks. Then last week, 2 billion dollars. You can tell this is an election year from the way these appropriation bills are passing. It will take the tax-payers fifty years to pay for the votes in this election.

"You know, you can't spend, say, 5 billion dollars in the old-fashioned way. I'll bet you couldn't put a strong man in the treasury warehouse full of $100 bills and give him a scoop shovel, and he couldn't shovel out that much money in the rest of his life.

"Used to, we couldn't spell a billion dollars, much less to realize it and count it or anything. But now we're a nation, we learn awful fast, and we won't be long now till we'll be aworkin' on the word 'trillion.' You'll read in the papers, 'Congress has just been asked to appropriate 2 trillion dollars to relieve the dependents of a race of people called Wall Streeters.' The paper will go further on to

say, 'This is a worthy cause, and no doubt this small appropriation will be made, as these are dependents of the once proud race…and after all, they're wards of the government.'"[12]

The New Deal was in full swing, and the federal government was fast becoming a major player in world finance and business. To accomplish its goals, the government needed two things: money and plans. Therefore, many new taxes were levied, especially on the rich, and Washington was just mangy with plans and planners.

In April of 1935, Will appeared on a number of weekly radio broadcasts for the Gulf Oil Company. He was in rare form on the subjects of taxes and plans in his broadcast of April 7th.

TAXES AND SPENDING

"Well, we cuss the lawmakers but I notice we're always perfectly willin' to share in any of the sums of money that they might distribute. We say it's wrong and unsound. We say that the way the government is run now is all nutty and that it's throwing money away. But anytime any is thrown our way, why we've never dodged it.

"Why it seems, if you don't believe in what Roosevelt is doing with this money, refuse it if it comes. Just say, 'No, it's government money, and it's tainted. And I don't believe in the government spending all this money, and hence I don't take any part of it.'

"Here's a man that maybe wants to pay his loan at the bank. Well, maybe the RFC loaned him the money. And naturally, all the banks say, 'I don't believe in the government spending all this money.' But when the man comes to pay his loan with the government money, they

don't say, 'No, I can't take it; I'll just carry you myself.' Boy, what a laugh that would be.

"So the only thing I see, for the fellow that don't believe in all this spending, is to not participate in receiving any of it. So this 5 billion dollars that they're starting in to spend, we all know that that's too much money. But until we refuse to take some of it, when it comes our way, we ain't got much right to holler.

"Now that brings us down to taxes. Boy, when you bring us down to taxes, you're going to hear a howl like a pet coon. Where's all this money coming from that the government is throwing away? Well, I don't know, but just offhand, I'd say it's coming from those that got it.

"So, the big yell comes nowadays from the big taxpayers. But, I bet you when the Pilgrims landed at Plymouth Rock and they had the whole of the American continent for themselves, and all they had to do to get an extra hundred and sixty acres was shoot another Indian, well, I bet you anything they kicked on the price of ammunition. I bet they said, 'What's this country coming to!' You know, what I mean...like we're doing now. 'What's this country coming to!??...that we have to spend a nickel for powder?' Of course, they got the lead back after they dissected the Indian.

"Ain't it funny that no matter what we pay...high taxes, low taxes, medium taxes, or no tax, anything...the yell is always the same, a hundred percent.

"Of course, we all know our government is costing us more than it's worth, but do you know of any other cheaper government that's running around? If you do, they'll sell you a ticket there anytime.

"Now you can try Russia. I was over there. There's no income tax in Russia, but there's no income. Now

Hitler...Hitler ain't got no sales tax...you know what I mean...but he ain't selling anything. Well, that's fine. Mussolini, you don't have to pay a poll tax to vote in Italy, you know...but nobody votes.

"So, the whole question is, 'How can we make such a holler on what the government wants to collect back from us?' The general contention is that nobody is spending any money but the government. Well, I guess that's right. The government is spending all the money.

"But, I figured out that it's a peculiar state of affairs that exists. Everybody that is doing better than they was three or four years ago has got it in for the president. But they don't seem to realize that they're doing better on the money that he's spending. Now we all know that the government is spending all this money and that's not a good state of affairs to exist. The country's in bad shape when there ain't nobody spending any money but the government.

"But it looks like we can't have everything like we want to. So the whole question with the government is: How much of this money, which we are asked to pay back to them in taxes, have they paid us? We must have got quite a little divvy of it some way or other...indirectly. Admitting, as everybody does, that the government is the only one spending money, then anything we're gettin' must come from them. It looks like an endless chain to me, only when it reaches our link, well, we don't want to cut any back into the kitty.

"But, I don't know what it's all about. This is just to kill time up here until something else comes on. I don't know any more about this thing than an economist does, and God knows, he don't know anything."[13]

Later in that same broadcast, Will told his audience to be ready the following week for the "Rogers Plan." He said everybody had a plan, so he figured he ought to have one. He told his listeners not to sign up with any other plans until he had a chance to tell them about his. But when April 14th rolled around, Will had failed to meet his assignment. He said he found out there was more to this planning deal than he had figured on. So he let his plan incubate a little longer and on the 14th he talked about the drought and the dust storms out West. But when April 21st rolled around, Will was ready with his

PLAN TO END ALL PLANS

"Well, it was a bad week for plans all around. I'm not going to get discouraged, though. In fact, these other failures...well, they've really given me confidence, you know...more hope that my plan will be a success.

"My plan, to state it in a nutshell, and...in fact, that's where all plans come from...and the nuts should never be cracked. But here is my plan in a nutshell. My plan is a plan to end all plans. It's to do away with all plans. That's what it is.

"There ain't but one place that a plan is any good and that's on paper. But the minute you get it off the sheet of paper and get it out in the air, and it blows away, that's all. Plans just don't work. If they're milk and honey to you, they are poison ivy to somebody else.

"But even if your plan don't work, it's no discredit, you know. Our own Saviour had a plan...in fact, ten of 'em. He left them to us, and he knew they'd help us...and we know they'll help us. He said, 'Love thy neighbor as thyself,' but I betcha there ain't two people in your block that's speaking to each other.

"We know there should be no war. We know that everybody should 'share the wealth.' We know all these things, but we just ain't going to do 'em, that's all.

"Now, Huey's [Senator Huey Long] *plan to 'share the wealth,' it's a marvelous idea. There ain't nothing wrong with the plan, only this one little defect: Nobody ain't going to share it with you, that's all.*

"Well, we take the case of Huey. Suppose Huey was asked to divide his publicity with the other ninety-five senators. Now what a fine thing. Say, 'Huey, we just want you to split this publicity with them,' see? Well, that would be just like getting J. P. Morgan to split what he had with a Navajo or something. Morgan would say, 'Well, why should I split with the Navajoes? I got nothing in common with the Navajoes.'

"Well, that's what Huey would say, 'Why should I split with the other ninety-five senators. I've got nothing in common with them.'

"Well, it just seems we got all these plans, but none of 'em pleases everybody. So my plan is when a senator or congressman…or even a man of great ability…comes to Washington with a plan, just send 'em to Russia. That's the home of plans, you know. They eat and sleep and drink plans in Russia. That's why there's starvation there, because you just can't digest a plan. It don't eat right. Everything in Russia is run by plans; everything here is run by accident.

"There's nothing in the world as common as an idea, and there's nothing in the world as hard to carry out as an idea. So let's all just kind of call a moratorium on plans. If the Republicans would forget their main plan, which is to get into the White House, and the Democrats would forget their main plan to stay in there, and if the

others...all these various third parties...would just look at their history which shows that none of them ever did get in there, why we'd all recover overnight.

"So if you hear a man expounding a plan over your radio, run, don't walk, to the nearest dial and tune him right into the ground, folks."[14]

Being true to his moderate nature, when things got too extreme, Will even defended the wealthy—well, sort of. In the April 28th broadcast, Will playfully skewered Secretary Morgenthau's latest tax plan.

SECRETARY MORGENTHAU'S TAX PLAN

"Do you remember my act on the radio last Sunday night? Well, even if you don't remember it, it don't matter very much. Fact, I'd about forgot it myself. But as well as I can remember it, I introduced a plan. It was a plan to end all plans. That's what it was.

"Well, it looked like it had the very opposite effect. This last week has been one of the biggest plan weeks the country has suffered in years .

"I presented facts and figures to show you that plans didn't work. Do you think that discouraged the planners? Not on your life. It just seemed to encourage them.

"Right on top of my advice to not plan, well, there came a plan from Secretary Morgenthau, who's secretary of the treasury. He come out with a plan to put a bigger and better tax on these big estates...an inheritance tax it is.

"On an estate of say $10 million, why the government will take about 90 percent of it, and then giving the offspring 10...after Mr. Morgenthau gets through with it. And then on estates of a 100 million, 200 million, a bil-

lion, and like that, well, the government just takes all of that and notifies the heirs…says, 'Your father died a pauper here today.' And 'He died a pauper here today, and he's being buried by the MEBA'…that is, the 'Millionaires' Emergency Burial Association.' It's a kind of a branch of the RFC.

"Now mind you, I don't hold any great grief for a man that dies and leaves millions and hundreds of millions and billions. I don't mean that. But I don't believe Mr. Morgenthau's plan will work. He gives these figures to show how much this new inheritance tax will bring in every year, that is, as long as the Democrats stay in. He seems to know just who's going to die each year. And how much they're going to leave. Now, brother, that's planning, ain't it, when you can figure out that!

"Now suppose, for instance, he's got scheduled J. P. Morgan to die on a certain year. And you can bet, if they can arrange it, they'll have him die while the Democrats are in…so they can get the benefit of that estate, see?

"Now, according to the plan, J. P. Morgan has got to die in order for Mr. Morgenthau to reach his quota for that year. Now while I think Mr. Morgan is a nice man. I never met him but once, but he was a very able, nice fellow…I don't hear from him but very seldom. I think his patriotism might compare with some of the rest of us, but whether he'd be patriotic enough to want to die on this year's schedule or not…just to make Morgenthau's boodget balance…I mean that's asking a good deal of a man, to just die right off, just so I can balance my boodget. He might be rather unreasonable and not want to do it. I say, old men is contrary…you know what I mean. And rich old men is awful contrary. They've had their own way so long.

"So in order for Mr. Morgenthau's plan to work out, he's got to bump these wealthy guys off, or something. Well, now, the government's doing everything else, you know, but there is a humane society."[15]

Will Rogers in *Down to Earth*

Regular folks have always had only two tax problems: making the money to pay them and getting them paid properly. It takes a rocket scientist to figure out a tax form and, when it is finished, even the IRS can't tell us if it's been done right. Will summed up the frustrations of the average taxpayer this way, *"Folks, this is income tax paying day. There is going to be no attempt at humor, for it would be mighty forced. No two can agree on what is deductible. When it's made out you don't know if you are crook or martyr. It's made more liars out of the American people than golf has."*[16]

Politicians today have to promise tax relief to the average family to get elected. But the relief they can actually give is a mere pittance. The reason for this is obvious. In the final analysis, it is the middle class that pays the bulk of the country's taxes. Even a small amount of relief given to the millions upon millions of middle class taxpayers represents a tremendous loss in revenue for the government. The promise of tax relief coupled with a balanced budget, so far, has been an impossible dream. Congress may cut taxes in one place but they raise them in another. Will said, *"When a party can't think of anything else they always fall back on Lower Taxes. It has a magic sound to a voter, just like Fairyland is spoken of, and dreamed of, by all children. But no child has ever seen it; neither has any voter ever lived to see the day when his taxes were lowered."*[17]

Will could make such a statement because he knew who pulled the strings in Washington.

LOBBYISTS

"Take the mess we're in now. Roosevelt wants recovery to start at the bottom. By a system of high taxes, he wants business to help the little fellow to get started and get some work, and then pay business back by buying things when he's back at work. Business says, 'Let business alone, and quit monkeying with us, and quit trying schemes, and we'll get everything going for you. And if we prosper, naturally the worker will prosper.'

"One wants recovery to start from the bottom, and the other wants it to start from the top. I don't know which is right. I've never heard of anybody suggesting that they might start it in the middle, so I hereby make that suggestion. To start recovery halfway between the two, because it's the middle class that does everything anyhow.[18]

"But we can't do that cause the middle class don't have a lobby. You see, every time Congress starts to tax

some particular industry, it rushes down with its main men and they scare 'em out of it. About the only way I see for 'em to do it, so it would be fair to everybody, would be for Congress to go into secret session, allow no telephones, no telegrams, no visitors, so no outside lobbyists can get at 'em, then tax everything they want to, and should tax, then announce, 'Boys, it's all over; there is no use shooting at us now.' As it is now, we are taxing everybody without a lobby.[19]

"If we have Senators and Congressmen that can't protect themselves against the evil temptations of lobbyists, we don't need to change our lobby, we need to change our representatives.

"Any person that can't spot a propagandist and lobbyist a mile away, must be a person so blind that they still think toupees are deceptive, and can't tell a hotel house detective from a guest."[20]

One of the things that bothers most of us is the abundance of commentators who constantly offer criticisms but no solutions. Will said, *"There is nothing as easy as denouncing…It don't take much to see that something is wrong, but it does take some eyesight to see what will put it right again."*[21]

Although, many of Will's "solutions" were submitted purely in jest, there were times when he seriously offered ideas that he felt had merit. This was the case with Will's belief in a National Sales Tax. Bear in mind, this method of taxation would be very hard to get past our friends in Washington today. It's intended to get money out of rich people.

NATIONAL SALES TAX

"Why don't they use a sales tax? That is the only fair

and just tax. Have no tax on necessary foods, and moderate priced necessary clothes, but put a tax on every other thing you buy or use. Then the rich fellow, who buys more and uses more, certainly has no way of getting out of paying his share.

"Put big taxes on everything of a luxury nature. You do that, and let the working man know that the rich have paid before they got it, and you will do more than any one thing to settle some of the unrest and dissatisfaction that you hear every day, by the every day people of this country. They know there is something wrong with taxation. No slick lawyer or income tax expert can get you out of a sales tax. If you don't want to pay any tax, just don't buy anything out of bare necessities and you pay no tax. But the minute you want a pair of those knee Golf Breeches, why let the Government pop it to you for about 50 cents on each dollar. That would cure you of looking funny.

"Taxation is about all there is to Government. People don't want their taxes lowered near as much as the politician tries to make you believe. People want JUST taxes, more than they want lower taxes. They want to know that every man is paying his proportionate share according to his wealth.[22]

"A tax paid on the day you buy is not as tough as asking you for it the next year when you are broke. It's worked on gasoline. It ought to work on Rolls Royces, cigarettes, lipstick, rouge and Coca-Cola.[23]

"And this idea, that a tax on something keeps anybody from buying it, is a lot of 'hooey.' They put it on gasoline all over the country and it hasn't kept a soul at home a single night or day. You could put a dollar a gallon on and still a pedestrian couldn't cross the street with safety without armor."[24]

10

APPLESAUCE

"I tell you Folks, all Politics is Applesauce."[1]

Given a cowboy's working environment, "Applesauce" is a pretty polite term to use when referring to politics. But Will had a strong sense of propriety. None of his acquaintances or loved ones could recall him ever using crude words. Other than an occasional "hell" or "damn," Will's swearing didn't amount to much. Sometimes he would really cut loose and call politics "bunk" or "hooey." Today we would consider this kind of restraint extremely prudish. In Will's day, it was seen as the mark of a gentleman.

Will liked a civilized brand of discourse that respected the other person's dignity and position. One wonders what he would have thought of a reporter asking the President of the United States what kind of underwear he wears—boxers or briefs? But even more to the point, what would he have thought of a public figure who felt compelled to answer such a question? Would Calvin Coolidge, Franklin Roosevelt, Harry Truman, or Dwight Eisenhower have been asked such a thing? And if asked, would they have answered? During Roosevelt's presidency, the press went so far as to avoid taking pictures of him while he was in his wheelchair. Given the prejudices of the times, they feared such photographs would cast doubt on the President's ability to lead. It was seen as unfair not only to the man but to his office. Would such restraint be exercised today? Not on your life.

This is not to say that our political past is devoid of social indiscretion and impolite language, or that the press didn't relish sensationalizing it. But in those days, political squabbling wasn't beamed instantaneously into every living room in America 365 days per year. Rarely did the public reach the kind of media overload that we all suffer now. But when it did, Will was there. Tiring of the mudslinging of the 1932 presidential campaign, Will, an advocate of civilized discourse, called for a time out.

> *"There should be a moratorium called on candidates' speeches. They have both called each other everything in the world they can think of. From now on they are just talking themselves out of votes.*
>
> *"The high office of President of the United States has degenerated into two ordinarily fine men being goaded on by their political leeches into saying things that, if they were in their right minds, they wouldn't think of saying.*
>
> *"This country is a thousand times bigger than any two men in it, or any two parties in it. This country has gotten where it is in spite of politics, not by the aid of it. That we have carried as much political bunk as we have and still survived shows we are a super-nation.*
>
> *"So, you two boys just get the weight of the world off your shoulders and go fishing. Now instead of calling each other names till next Tuesday, why you can do everybody a big favor by going fishing and you will be surprised, but the old United States will keep right on running while you boys are sitting on the bank.*
>
> *"Then, come back next Wednesday and we will let you know which one is the lesser of the two evils of you."*[2]

Debunking politics was Will's stock and trade. To expose the "applesauce" of it, he once honored a request by Theodore Roosevelt, Jr., to speak in support of Ogden Mills, a Republican who was running for Congress. But Will's speech hardly amounted to an endorsement. With tongue firmly in cheek, he supported his candidate, attacked the opponent, and retained his own neutrality.

WILL'S FIRST POLITICAL SPEECH

"Ladies and Gentlemen. I have spoken in all kinds of joints...from the homes of the rich on 5th Avenue to telling jokes in Sing Sing. But this is my first crack at a political speech. And I hope it flops. I don't want it to get over. If it did it might lead me into politics and up til now I've tried to live honest.

"Now a great many think that I was sent here to speak by my candidate's opponent. That is not the case. I don't know him. But he must be a scoundrel. For what I have read of politics, every opponent is a scoundrel and a tool of the interests.

"Now, I have just investigated tonight, before coming on the platform, and found out which party my candidate was running on...as I think every speaker should be familiar with every phase of his subject. Now I don't know or have never met my candidate, and for that reason, I am more apt to say something good of him than anyone else.

"I was asked to do this by one of the Roosevelt boys. And you know that nobody could ever refuse a Roosevelt. Now I find a peculiar case in my candidate. Most people take up politics through necessity or as a last resort, but I find this guy was wealthy before he went in. Not as wealthy as he is now but...still...rich! That's what he

went in for, To protect what he had. As they say, 'There's honor among 'em.'

"His principle political handicap is that he was educated at Harvard. But I understand that he has forgotten most of that, so that brings him back to earth. Before going to Washington this last term he was slumming for four terms in the state legislature in Albany. On account of his wealth, he is the only man in the campaign that you can accept a cigar from and smoke it yourself. He is the only man in congress who owns his own dress suit. He is the only politician outside of Henry Cabot Lodge who can get in the front door of a 5th Avenue home without delivering something. I thank you."[3]

WILL ROGERS FOR PRESIDENT

People were always getting a wild idea to run Will for president. But he never took it seriously. When someone made the suggestion in 1928, Will wrote, "*There was a piece in the paper this morning where somebody back home was seriously proposing me for President. Now when that was done as a joke it was all right, but when it's done seriously it's just pathetic. We are used to having everything named as Presidential candidates, but the country hasn't quite got to the professional comedian stage."*[4]

Election time in 1932 found Will very busy. He was invited to speak at both the Democratic and Republican conventions that year and was well received at both. At the Democratic Convention, the "Will Rogers for President" idea came up again. He even garnered a twenty-two delegate nomination as "Oklahoma's Favorite Son." His candidacy was short-lived, however.

"Politics ain't on the level. I was only in 'em for an hour but in that short space of time somebody stole 22 votes from me. I was sitting there in the press stand asleep and wasn't bothering a soul, when they woke me up and said Oklahoma had started me on the way to the White House with 22 votes.

"I thought to myself, well, there is no use going there this late in the morning, so I dropped off to sleep again, and that's when somebody touched me for my whole roll, took the whole 22 votes, didn't even leave me a vote to get breakfast on.

"Course I realize now that I should have stayed awake and protected my interest, but it was the only time I had ever entered national politics and I didn't look for the boys to nick me so quick. Besides, no man can listen to thirty-five nominating speeches and hold his head up. And I am sure some of these that did the nominating can never hold theirs up again.

"So, now what am I? Just another ex-Democratic Presidential candidate. There's thousands of 'em. Well, the whole thing has been a terrible lesson to me and there's nothing to do but start in and live it down."[5]

This idea of running Will just wouldn't go away. When people started making serious overtures about drafting him into the race, some very prominent folks took notice. Presidential hopeful Franklin D. Roosevelt wrote Will a few weeks before the convention and said, "Don't forget you are a Democrat by birth, training and tough experience and I know you won't get mixed up in any fool movement to make the good old Donkey chase his own tail and give the Elephant a chance to win the race."[6]

Franklin was just checking on Will's intentions, but he

really had nothing to worry about. Will said he much preferred maintaining his neutrality and taking his shots from the sidelines. Little shots like, *"I'm just trying to tell you the truth here. You see, I never got mixed up in politics, therefore I am able to tell the truth. No...and I don't belong to any organized political party either...I am a Democrat."* [7]

Actually, Will never officially claimed to be a Democrat or a Republican. He always made a joke out of it. Many labeled him a Democrat but he explained, *"I keep saying I'm a Democrat, but I ain't. I just pretend to be 'cause Democrats are funny and I'm supposed to be."*[8]

When it came to politics, Will contended that truth was the rarest and most dangerous of all commodities. He said, *"I guess the truth can hurt you worse in an election than about anything that could happen to you."* [9] To elaborate on the subject, Will found humor in a new invention of his day: Scopolamine, or

TRUTH SYRUM

"Say, we have a discoverer out here in California, a Dr. House of Texas, who has invented a serum called Scopolamine, a thing that when injected into you will make you tell the truth, at least for a while, anyway. They tried it on a male movie star in Hollywood and he told his right salary and his press agent quit him. They then tried it on a female movie staress and she recalled things back as far as her first husband's name. Their only failure to date has been a Los Angeles real estate agent. They broke three needles trying to administer the stuff to him and it turned black the minute it touched him, so they had to give him up. He sold Dr. House three lots before they got out of the operating room.

"It really is a wonderful thing though, and if it could be brought into general use it would no doubt be a big aid

to humanity. But it will never be, for already the politicians are up in arms against it. It would ruin the very foundation on which our political government is run.

"If you ever injected truth into politics you have no politics." [10]

In Will's day, conventions and elections were the three-ring circuses of politics—and Will was their ringmaster! Many decisions were made in smoke-filled rooms. But unlike the orchestrated media events we have today, the conventions were not neatly packaged infomercials. They could get ugly! Bitter public battles were waged as each party selected its candidates. Voters, without television, had to be reached through thousands of committed volunteers, building coalitions on the grass roots level and hoping for political favors later. All the fundamentals of the process are still with us today, making Will's comments as timely as ever.

ELECTIONS

"So much money is being spent on these campaigns that I doubt if either man, as good as they are, is worth what it will cost to elect them. [11]

"Now you take this Democratic Party, I think it could be made to pay, but the present owners have absolutely no business with it. Under present management they have killed off more good men than grade crossings have. [12]

"And the Republicans? Republicans take care of the big money, for big money takes care of them. [13]

"It takes nerve to be a Democrat, but it takes money to be a Republican. [14]

"Now take Democratic presidents. They're all big on plans. Somebody had a plan one time to teach hogs birth control. Now, it's a habit with 'em…and you can go out

and find a deer quicker than you can a hog these days. It was all a fine plan…and well carried out. We wanted to raise commodity prices. We wanted to give the farmer a profit, the same as the manufacturer, you know.

"Well now, somebody had a plan to plow under every third acre of wheat…remember that?…then the wind came along and blew out the other two acres.

"But that's one thing about Republican presidents. They never went in much for plans. They only had one plan and it says…uh…'Boys, my head is turned, take it while you can.'[15]

"But you know, a flock of Democrats will replace a mess of Republicans. It won't mean a thing. They will go in like all the rest of 'em. Go in on promises and go out on alibis."[16]

Isn't there something to the argument that we get the kind of politicians we deserve? As voters, we are fickle in the extreme. We will overlook a lot of political shenanigans as long as our interests are being protected. If the job is secure and the economy strong, we are satisfied with the status quo. But let things get a little shaky and politicians look out! Will said,

"Everybody figures Politics according to what they have accumulated during the last couple of years. Maybe you haven't earned as much as you did a few years ago, because you haven't worked near as hard, but all you look at is the old balance sheet and if it's in the RED why his Honor the President is in the alley as far as you are concerned.[17] *A voter just goes to the polls and if he has got a dollar you stay in, and if he ain't got a dollar, you go out. The memory of a voter is about as long as a billy goat."*[18]

If extraterrestrials were to land on this planet, no doubt we could explain a lot of our math, science, and engineering to them. But explaining human behavior, especially surrounding politics, would be a different matter. If you project our unexplainable behavior as individuals onto a grand scale, you have politics. From the beginning of our history, this effort to get along with each other has brought out our strengths and our weaknesses, our nobility and our pettiness. Explaining to an extraterrestrial that human beings don't have just one quality, but many different ones, often in direct contradiction with each other, would be like trying to explain how Democrats and Republicans are just alike but completely different at the same time – which they are. Will knew this and spent his whole career playing with the concept.

DEMOCRATS AND REPUBLICANS

"Lots of people never know the difference between a Republican and a Democrat. Well, I will tell you how to tell the difference. The Democrats are the ones who split. That's the only way you can tell them from the Republicans. If the Democrats never split in their lives there would be no such thing as a Republican.[19]

"Now, Republicans have always been the party of big business, and the Democrats of small business, so you just take your pick. The Democrats had their eye on a dime, and the Republicans on a dollar.[20]

"You see, a Republican moves slowly. They are what we call conservatives. A conservative is a man who has plenty of money and doesn't see any reason why he shouldn't always have plenty of money. A Democrat is a fellow who never had any, but doesn't see any reason why he shouldn't have some. So the idea of closing a bank, of your

own free will and accord, is as foreign to a Republican as selling stock, which you don't own, is foreign to a Democrat. It's not that the Democrat's conscience would hurt him, it's just that he never thought of the thing.[21]

"A Democrat never adjourns. He is born, becomes of voting age and starts right in arguing over something, and his first political adjournment is his date with the undertaker.[22]

"If you ask a Republican, he'll tell you that Republicans were responsible for radio, telephones, baths, automobiles, savings accounts, enforcement, workmen living in houses and a living wage for Senators.

"The Democrats brought on war, pestilence, debts, disease, boll weevil, gold teeth, need of farm relief, suspenders, floods, and famines.[23]

"The whole trouble with the Republicans is their fear of an increase in income tax, especially on higher incomes. They speak of it almost like a national calamity. I really believe if it come to a vote whether to go to war with England, France and Germany combined, or raise the rate on incomes of over $100,000, they would vote war.[24]

"That's one thing about a Democrat. They never are as serious as the Republicans. They been out of work so long they got used to it.

"The Democrats take the whole thing as a joke and the Republicans take it serious, but run it like a joke. So there's not much difference."[25]

Now that we've let Will define Democrats and Republicans, let's let him further confuse those extraterrestrials by explaining congressmen and senators.

CONGRESSMEN AND SENATORS

"I received a wire from a Congressman friend of mine, who wants a copy of some fool thing I wrote, to read into the Congressional Record. Now, I feel pretty good about that. That's the highest praise that a humorist can have, is to get your stuff into the Congressional Record. Just think, my name will be right in there, alongside of Huey Long's, and all those other big humorists.

"You see, ordinarily you got to work your way up as a humorist and first get into Congress. Then you work on up into the Senate, and then if your stuff is funny enough it goes into the Congressional Record. But for an outsider to get in there as a humorist without having served his apprenticeship in either the House or the Senate, why that's…mind you, I'm not bragging, but by golly I feel pretty big about it.

"Did I ever tell you, I don't know whether I did, or not, about the first time I ever had any of my stuff in that daily? Well, I had written some fool thing, and it pertained to the bill that they were arguing…I mean, that they was kidding about…in the Senate. So, some Senator read my little article, and anything a Senator reads, goes into the Record. So another Senator rose, and said, as they always do, if you have ever seen them: 'Does the gentleman yield?'

"They always say that. They call each other gentlemen in there, but the tone that they put on the words, it would be more appropriate, you know the way they say 'gentleman', it would sound better if he come right out and said: 'Does the coyote from Maine yield?' That's about the way it sounds, you know; he says 'gentleman,' but it kind of sounds like 'coyote.'

"Then the man says, 'I yield.' For if he don't, the other

guy will keep on talking anyhow. So the 'coyote' from Maine says: 'I yield to the polecat from Oregon.' He don't say 'polecat,' but he says 'gentleman' in such a way, that it is almost like 'polecat.'

"Well, anyhow, that's the way they do it. They are very polite in Congress.

"But there are some exceptions. Did you hear about this? It sure did kick up some excitement. Senator Moses called the other Senators 'sons of wild jackasses.' Well, if you think it made the Senators hot, you wait till you see what happens when the jackasses hear how they have been slandered.[26]

"But I must get back to my story. When this Senator read my offering, the other Senator said—after all the yielding was over—the other Senator said, 'I object to the remarks of a professional joke maker being put in the Congressional Record!'

"You know, meaning me. He was takin' a dig at me, see? They didn't want any outside fellers contributin' I guess.

"Well, he had me wrong. Compared to those fellows in Congress, I'm just an amateur. And the thing about my jokes is that they don't hurt anybody. You can take 'em, or leave 'em. You know what I mean. You can say they are not funny, or they are terrible, or they are good, or whatever it is, but they don't do any harm. But with Congress, every time they make a joke, it's a law!

"And every time they make a law, it's a joke!"[27]

Because of our system of checks and balances, the relationship between our legislators and our presidents has always been a contentious one. Will liked the fellows on the legislative side of our government but his sympathies seemed to lie with the executive branch. He gave the presidents their fair share of grief, but, more often than not, he saw the presidents as inspiring and the legislators as humorous.

Senator Pat Harrison and Will Rogers

"No wonder presidents don't trust Senators. Why, distrust of the Senate by Presidents started with Washington, who wanted to have 'em court-martialed. Jefferson proposed life imprisonment for 'em, old Andy Jackson said 'To hell will 'em,' and got his wish. Lincoln said the Lord must have hated 'em, for he made so few of 'em.

"Roosevelt whittled a big stick and beat on 'em for six years. Taft just laughed at 'em and grew fat. They drove

Wilson to an early grave. Coolidge never let 'em know what he wanted, so they never knew how to vote against him, and Mr. Hoover took 'em serious, thereby making his only political mistake.[28]

"Mr. Hoover didn't get results because he asked Congress to do something. This fellow, Franklin Roosevelt, he just sends a thing up there every morning. He says, 'Here's your menu, you guys. What are you going to order?' And he tells them just what they're going to have. Now Mr. Roosevelt, he never, never scolds them. You know, he kids them. Congress is really just children that's never grown up, that's all they are.[29]

"Now, I like to make little jokes and kid about the Senators and Congressmen. They are a kind of a never ending source of amusement, amazement, and Discouragement. But the Rascals, when you meet 'em face to face and know 'em, they are mighty nice fellows. It must be something in the office that makes 'em so honery sometimes. When you see what they do officially you want to shoot 'em, but when one looks at you and grins so innocently, why you kinder want to kiss him."[30]

Today our presidents are so embattled from the moment they take office that it is rare for them to have a comfortable relationship with their critics in the media. This was not the case with Will. He often expressed his admiration for Teddy Roosevelt's vigorous lifestyle and Franklin Delano Roosevelt's take-charge attitude. Many presidents Will admired returned the compliment. Woodrow Wilson commented, "His remarks are not only humorous but illuminating."[31] Franklin Delano Roosevelt said, "The first time that I fully realized Will Rogers' exceptional and deep understanding of political and social problems was when he came back from his long European trip a good many years ago. While I had discussed European matters with many others, both American and foreign, Will Rogers' analysis of affairs abroad was not only more interesting but proved to be more accurate than any other I had heard."[32]

Will's little jabs at these men were always tempered by respect. But when he criticized the two candidates in the 1932 election (Hoover and Roosevelt) by suggesting that they "go fishin'," he received a lot of letters from people who thought he had shown disrespect toward the office of the presidency. Will responded to his readership with the following:

> *"Now I poke my little fun at the Presidents, but I don't care who you are, you haven't got any more respect for the man and the office than I have. I think Mr. Hoover knows what I think of him personally and how I admire him as a man.*
>
> *"Mr. Coolidge, who I made a living out of for years, had no greater and still has no greater admirer and staunch supporter of his splendid qualities, than I am.*
>
> *"Now this Mr. Roosevelt that's coming in, he is a particular friend of mine for many years standing, he and his whole family, but I have got to start in now pretty soon making a living out of the fool things he and those Democrats will do, and I am not worried, I know they will do plenty of 'em.*
>
> *"I generally give the party in power, whether Republican or Democrat, the more digs because they are generally doing the country more damage, and besides I don't think it is fair to jump too much on the fellow who is down. He is not working, he is only living in hopes of getting back in on the graft in another four years, while the party in power is drawing a salary to be knocked."*[33]

Being president of the United States has to be one of the most thankless jobs around. It makes you wonder why anyone would want it. Presidents have to be extremely thick-skinned, patriotic, and perhaps a little bit crazy. If the intensity of the job gets much worse, all of our truly talented people will stop seeking the office. Will said, *"They do love to be President. It's the toughest job in the world, but there is always 120 million applicants."*[34] Every one of us thinks we can do the job better than the person we've elected. Will knew better. Here's a quick little survey of how Will felt about the office of the presidency and some of the occupants of the White House.

PRESIDENTS

"Now let's take George Washington...of course, he was great...he was the Father of our Country on account of having no children. He was a surveyor and he owned half of Virginia, because he surveyed his own lines. He was a general on our side because England wouldn't make him one on theirs. He was a politician and a gentleman...that is a rare combination.[35]

"Thomas Jefferson was the most far-sighted Democrat in either his or any other time and they named the Democratic party after him. That is, he was for the poor but was himself of the rich.[36] *Jefferson sitting up there on that hill believed in equality for all. But he didn't divide up that hill with any poor Democrats.*[37] *This Jefferson seemed to be the only Democrat in History with any kind of business ability.*[38]

"Now, Abraham Lincoln ?...He made a wonderful speech one time: 'That this Nation under God, shall have a new Birth of Freedom, and that Government of the People, by the People, for the People, shall not perish from

this earth.'

"Now, every time a Politician gets in a speech, he digs up this Gettysburg quotation. He recites it every Decoration day and practices the opposite the other 364 days.[39]

"Calvin Coolidge kept his mouth shut. That was such a novelty among Politicians that it just swept the Country. Originality will be rewarded in any line.[40]

"Herbert Hoover! I always did want to see him elected. I wanted to see how far a competent man could go in politics. It had never been tried before.[41]

"And now we come to Franklin Delano Roosevelt. This Roosevelt is a mighty fine human man. Sometimes I think he is too nice a fellow to be mixed up in all this politics.[42] *And, you know, an awful lot of folks are predicting Roosevelt's downfall, not only predicting but praying. We are a funny people. We elect our Presidents, be they Republican or Democrat, then go home and start daring 'em to make good.*[43] *And ain't this odd, everybody that is making money has it in for Roosevelt. You will have to explain that one yourself.*[44]

"America is just like an insane asylum, there is not a soul in it will admit they are crazy. Roosevelt being the warden at the present time, us inmates know he is the one that's cuckoo.[45]

"But we're just wonderful with our presidents. When the sun is shining we cheer 'em, and let it start raining and if they don't furnish some umbrellas and gooloshes, boy, we give him the boot right then.[46]

"All in all it's a tough life, this thing of being President and trying to please everybody. (Well not exactly everybody but enough to re-elect.)"[47]

You'll notice when Will is speaking of specific individuals he is always kind in his approach. He saves his more cutting remarks for when he talks about politicians or institutions in general. "*I tell ya, once a man wants to hold public office, he is absolutely no good for honest work.*[48] *It's getting so if a man wants to stand well socially he can't afford to be seen with either the Democrats or the Republicans.*[49] *Ain't it funny how many hundreds of thousands of soldiers we can recruit with nerve. But we just can't find one politician in a million with backbone.*"[50]

Will could get heated about some issues. But most of the time, Will didn't take his politicians or their "applesauce" too seriously. He said, "*I don't make jokes, folks. I just watch the govm't and I report the facts.*[51] *Besides, with every public man we have elected doing comedy, I don't see much of a chance for a comedian to make a living. I am just on the verge of going to work. They can do more funny things naturally, than I can think of to do purposely.*"[52]

11

"...AS LONG AS GRASS GROWS AND WATER FLOWS"

"...They said, 'You can have this ground as long as grass grows and water flows.' On account of its being a grammatical error, the Government didn't have to live up to it. Now they have moved the Indians and they settled the whole thing by putting them on land where the grass won't grow and the water won't flow."[1]

When it comes to race relations and advocating for minorities, Will was most articulate when addressing the plight of his own group, American Indians. This is understandable since Will felt the sting of racism early in life. In a 1935 interview by David Randolph Milsten, the famous cowboy movie star, Tom Mix, related the following story about his early days working with Will in Wild West shows: "One night, [at Madison Square Garden] Bill came to me and said, 'Tom, there are some keen looking girls out in the boxes and I am going to throw my rope toward 'em to see if I can't get a play out of 'em.'...That night when Bill came into the room where we were bunked, I noticed he was looking low in spirits. He walked toward me, kicking the floor, his head down and his hat well back on his head...I asked him if anything was wrong, and he replied, 'I heard those girls say that they was strong for me till they read on the program that I was an Indian, and one of 'em said she could stand being entertained by the darkest inhabitant in Africa, but an Indian went against her nature.'"[2] A young Will Rogers never forgot how that felt and it influenced his racial attitudes for the rest of his life.

But this is not to say that Will was perfect or a picture of political correctness as we define it today. He was a product of his times. Will's son, Jim, once told me that his father occasionally used the racial epithets that were common in his day in the course of normal conversation. But he didn't recall his father ever using them vindictively or often.

Much has changed since the days of Will Rogers. For example, in Will's youth, "coon songs" were very popular. These songs promoted an image of the black man as a clown-like Jim Crow figure: shiftless, lazy, and always into trouble. They were recorded by black and white artists alike, and a wide variety of people saw them as funny. Will, while in his teens, acquired quite a repertoire of them. After delivering cattle to the Kansas City railhead, he would scour the stores in town, looking for the sheet music of the latest hits. He would buy as many as he could afford, bring them back home, find someone to play the piano, and sing them, to the delight of his friends. Today, such a performance would be met with derision. But this was roughly a hundred years ago. People commonly indulged in humor about ethnic and religious groups different from their own. Many ethnic actors and comedians built lucrative careers by developing stereotypical characters that made fun of their own groups. Some of this humor showed an ability to laugh at oneself. Some of it was cruel and degrading. Very little of it would be acceptable today.

But don't be misled. Although Will was the product of a period we consider less enlightened on such matters, he scores very high points when it comes to racial acceptance and religious tolerance. Surrounded by the prejudices of his day, he was far ahead of his time, and his career proved it.

Will starred in many movies during the 1930s that used black actors. One of his favorite costars was Stepin Fetchit. Fetchit always played a dimwitted character who kowtowed to white people. His character was a product of the racial attitudes of his day. But Stepin Fetchit and other black actors who shared the screen with Will Rogers should be appreciated in the context of history. The country was in the depth of the Great Depression, and many actors were out of work. Studios were failing, so moviemakers were taking aim at the largest audiences possible: white audiences. This hit African-American actors especially hard. Very few roles were offered, and when they were, they were extremely limited. It was a given that a black actor could appear with a leading star only as a servant, laborer, or domestic, with no spoken lines.

Will was the biggest box office draw of his day. He not only used black actors but gave them featured roles with speaking parts. In John Ford's *Judge Priest* (1934), Will played a small-town judge in Kentucky just after the Civil War. In the course of the story, Will's character shared various key scenes of both dialogue and singing with Stepin Fetchit, Hattie McDaniel, and other black actors. Although considered small potatoes today, in its time, this was revolutionary. Casting black actors in speaking roles was so unusual that Will received numerous letters from disgruntled southerners, one of which read partially as follows:

"*Judge Priest* is far, very far from being a true picture of the South of that period that it depicts (or any other period)...The Negroes kept, and still do, their places as servants, respectful and obedient, never appearing in public except in caps and aprons (in other words, uniforms); the women with clean dresses, caps and aprons, the men wearing a white coat, all the time keeping a respectful silence. The South of that day was known for its culture, and I know not in history of a Southern jurist manifesting so great ignorance as Judge Priest manifested…It is a pity those who do not know anything about the 'Old South' should assign you to a part that is destined to ruin you with Southern people."[3]

Hattie McDaniel, Gladys Wells, Melba Brown and Will Rogers in *Judge Priest*

My favorite story regarding Will and Stepin Fetchit will have to be categorized as folklore, because I received it secondhand. In May of 1995, after I had performed for a conference of prominent scientists in Norman, Oklahoma, one of the participants told me that his father had met Will Rogers. Will was filming a movie in Northern California shortly before he died (most likely *Steamboat Round the Bend*) and this man's father owned a ranch in the area.

When Will came into town, he asked, "Where's my costar?," meaning Stepin Fetchit. They explained that since Fetchit wasn't allowed to stay in the "whites only" hotel in town, he had gone out to the ranch. If it was good enough for Stepin it was good enough for Will. He got a car and drove out. My scientist friend told me that his father's favorite story was about the time he, Stepin Fetchit, and Will Rogers sat around his kitchen table, telling their biggest lies and exaggerations until 3:00 in the morning. When it came time to call it a night, Rogers and Fetchit retired to the barn.

I intended to catch up with this gentleman later in the evening to get his name and further details, but I regret that I never saw him again. But his story gave me a good example of how Will's famous quote, "I never met a man I didn't like," crossed racial barriers. He saw all of us as about the same and deserving of respect and friendship. When pleading for relief for flood victims in 1927, Will said to a public blind to the plight of poor blacks, *"When you talk about poor people that have been hit by this flood, look at the thousands and thousands of negroes that never did have much, but now it's washed away. You don't want to forget that water is just as high up on them as it is if they were white. The Lord so constituted everybody that no matter what color you are you require about the same amount of nourishment."*[4]

When asked about his own roots, Will was obviously proud of his Indian ancestry. The Cherokee people had a rich history and Will wanted everyone to know it. He said, *"My father was one-eighth Cherokee Indian...and my mother, she was a quarter-blood Cherokee. Now, I never got far enough in arithmetic to figure out just how much 'Injun' that makes me, but I tell ya, there ain't nothing' in my whole life of which I am more proud of than my Cherokee blood. You see, my ancestors didn't come on the Mayflower, but they met the boat.*"[5]

Although the other side of Will's ancestry was a mix of Welsh, Scotch, and Irish, he wasn't proud of his white ancestor's treatment of the Indians. He said,

> *"Our record with the Indians is going to go down in history. It is going to make us mighty proud of it in the future when our children of ten more generations read of what we did to them. Every man in our history that killed the most Indians has got a statue built for him. The only difference between the Roman gladiators and the Pilgrims was that the Romans used a lion to cut down their native population, and the Pilgrims had a gun. The Romans didn't have no gun; they just had to use a lion."*[6]

In a radio broadcast of April 7, 1935, you may recall, Will made the statement, *"I bet you when the Pilgrims landed at Plymouth Rock and they had the whole of the American continent for themselves, and all they had to do to get an extra hundred and sixty acres was shoot another Indian. Well, I bet you anything they kicked on the price of ammunition."*[7] In response to that comment, he got a letter from the Provincetown Chamber of Commerce complaining about his supposed inaccuracy regarding the Pilgrims' actual landing place. In the broadcast the following week, Will took the opportunity to poke a little fun at Provincetown's civic pride, deflate the legacy of the Pilgrims, and score a few points for the Indians.

PILGRIMS

> *"On last Sabbath evening, I referred to the Pilgrims landing on Plymouth Rock. Well, boy, you ought to wait*

'til I heard from New England. I split New England just wide open. It seems there's a town up there called Provincetown, and they have adopted a slogan which says, 'Don't be misled by history or any other unreliable source. Here's the place where the Pilgrims landed. This is by unanimous vote of the Chamber of Commerce of Provincetown. Provincetown has been made the official landing place of the Pilgrims. Any Pilgrim landing in any other place was not official.'

"Now in the first place, I don't think that this argument I have created up there is so terribly important. The argument that New England has got to settle in order to pacify the rest of America is, 'Why were they allowed to land anywhere?' That's what we want to know. As a race there has never been any comparison between the Pilgrim and an Indian. Now I hope my Cherokee blood is not making me prejudiced. I want to be broadminded, but I am sure that it was only the extreme generosity of the Indians that allowed the Pilgrims to land. Suppose we reversed the case. Do you reckon the Pilgrims would have ever let the Indians land? Yeah, what a chance! What a chance! The Pilgrims wouldn't even allow the Indians to live after the Indians went to the trouble of letting 'em land.

"Well anyhow, the Provincetown officials, they sent me a lot of official data, that when the Pilgrims landed they found some corn that the Indians had stored and that the Pilgrims were about starved and that they ate the Indians' corn. And they claim that the corn was stored at Provincetown. You see, the minute the Pilgrims landed they got full of the corn and then they shot the Indians, perhaps because they hadn't stored more corn. I don't know.

"Of course…they'd always pray. That's one thing about a Pilgrim. He would pray, mostly for more Indian corn. You've never in your life seen a picture of one of the old Pilgrims praying when he didn't have a gun right by the side of him. That was to see that he got what he was praying for."[8]

Since Will was of both Indian and pioneer stock, his people were close to the earth. He held to the principles of a rural life. But at the same time, he embraced the inventions of the twentieth century—radio, movies, and especially aviation. This made him a man of two worlds. Although he found all the new developments exciting, he looked at so-called progress with a skeptical eye. He had more faith in old ways and simpler people.

The country was in deep crisis. Not only was the economy in shambles, but the weather wasn't cooperating either. It was the dust bowl years: four straight years of solid drought. Even though Will made jokes, he deeply resented seeing his beautiful open range just blowing away on the wind. And he wasn't one to sit idly by and not say anything about it. Will was at the top of his form in his radio broadcast of April 1935, when he delivered an environmental message that we are only now starting to take seriously.

PIONEERS, DUST BOWLS, AND PHARAOHS

"Well, now, I've been reading a lot about this dust and been reading a lot in history, and that's how every civilization since time began in the whole world has been covered up. It's been this dust. It's a terrible thing to happen to those people that are out there in the Middle West where it is happening. But on the other hand, it's a great tribute to feel that the Lord feels that you have a civi-

lization that is so more advanced than the rest of civilization that it is the first place to be buried under.

"Now you see, my wife and daughter has just returned from a trip down in Egypt, and they went way up the Nile and went in at Luxor and went way down, she told me, hundreds of feet down in underground, that had been covered by the dust and storms of centuries and centuries, to see old King Tut and Ramses and the old Pharaoh's tomb. That was a great civilization,...buried in the blowing sand. See?...it's all been covered up because they plowed under ground that they shouldn't never plowed under in the first place,...and they cut down the trees that should never have been cut down anyhow."

Will had a bone to pick with people he felt were abusing the land. In the early days of the westward expansion, there were no laws governing land use and no concept of conservation. The idea of treating lumber as a renewable resource hadn't crossed anybody's mind. Trees were clear cut and nothing was planted in their place. The destruction of millions of buffalo happened in much the same way, and the Indian side of Will didn't like the wasteful side of his European brethren. He continues,

"You know, we're always talking about pioneers and what great folks the old pioneers were. Well, I think if we just stopped and looked at history in the face, we'd see that the old pioneer wasn't a thing in the world but a guy that wanted something for nothing. He was a guy that wanted to live off of everything that nature had done. He wanted to cut a tree down that didn't cost him anything, but he never did plant one. He wanted to plow up the

land that should have been left to grass. We're just now learning that we can rob from nature the same way as we can rob from an individual. But all he had was an ax, and a plow, and a gun, and he just went out and lived off nature. He thought it was nature he was living off of, but it was really future generations.

"Now Roosevelt, do you remember, here a couple of years ago? He suggested planting millions of trees in all the dry regions. He said every so many miles we'll put a row of trees clear across the country. Well, the Republicans had one of the best laughs they've had since 1928 when they read that. 'Imagine the government going into the tree planting business.' What a nut idea. And it was nutty. It was so nutty that it will be about ten or fifteen years before they'll be compelled to do it. That's how nutty it was.

"And another one of his ideas when he took the young boys off the roads and off the streets and put them in these CCC Camps and had 'em all planting some little trees. The press had a big laugh. They called them 'sapling planters.' 'Look at these young kids. They got 'em all planting saplings.' Well, if the sapling planters had started in about the time the Republicans took over the government from Grover Cleveland, we'd today be able to see the sun.

"But now wait a minute, you Democrats. It wasn't all Republicans that did this. The old Democrat had an ax, too. In fact, that's all the Democrat had had for years, is an ax. He ain't had nothing else. He's practically had to live off of an ax. Of course until here lately, he traded his ax for a post office. He's living off the post office now.

"But I must get back from these political parties and get back to civilization, for there's nothing in common

between politics and civilization. There ain't nothing in common between those two at all."

Will didn't seem to think either Democrats or Republicans were all that great when it came to the environment. The Industrial Revolution knew few party lines. At the same time it created great fortunes, it also created jobs. Naturally, both parties could get behind that agenda. But, in the face of all the "progress" he was witnessing, Will felt compelled to gently remind us that past civilizations had plundered the land beyond its tolerance, and although we may think of ourselves as special, maybe we are not.

"If history has shown the Lord does bury each succeeding civilization, and buries them in accordance to the advancement of the people in that neighborhood, I feel proud that I come from that particular Middle West belt. I know that William Allen White of Kansas feels proud, and Amon Carter of Texas feels proud.

"If a civilization had to be buried as it becomes advanced enough, well, we feel proud that we're the ones to be plowed under first, that's all. In years to come the archeologist...I hope I've got that right...I say archeologist. The archeologist will dig and find Claremore, Oklahoma, and people will come there to the ruins and dig down and say, 'Here lied a civilization.'

"Well, then later on they'll unearth the state capitol. And then eventually as Washington is covered up (on account of it's being the least civilized, it will be the last place to be covered up) they will excavate in there and find the old Capitol and decipher some of the old hieroglyphics...you know, what people of those days humorously called laws. And they'll come from the four corners

> *of the earth to see what queer race lived there. And they'll find places called banks where the money changers were...men who in those ancient days lived by interest alone. Oh, there ain't no telling to what all they won't...*[Alarm clock rings]*...Ah, wait a minute here. There ain't no telling. Shoot, I just got started telling you what all they was going to dig up in Washington. Well, good-bye and good luck to you."*[9]

No doubt Will's Indian blood had something to do with his love of the land. He felt the land was sacred and that we should live in harmony with it. He said, *"Have you noticed? The animals are having a great year. The grass was never higher, flowers were never more in bloom, trees are throwing out an abundance of shade for us to loaf under. Everything the Lord has a hand in is going great, but the minute you notice anything that is in any way under the supervision of man, why it's 'cockeyed.'"*[10]

After living on the land for thousands of years, the Indians had left it relatively unscathed. Because of the Indians' limited technology, nature always had the upper hand. But in the few hundred years since the arrival of the Europeans, all of that was changing. Will had his roots in these two vastly different cultures – people whose religious beliefs regarding humanity and nature couldn't have been more polarized. In most cases, the Europeans felt that God put human beings on earth to dominate it, to impose order on nature. The Indians were more inclined to see nature as a great mystery, to be adapted to rather than figured out and subdued.

There is an Indian ethic that states, "Make your decisions with an eye toward how they will affect your people seven generations from now." Earlier in this chapter, Will wonders how our children of "ten more generations" will judge our treatment of the Indians. Concern for the kind of world he would leave to those children contributed to many of Will's opinions about the stampede of progress that he was witnessing.

While Americans have made some changes since that time, we remain the most rampant consumers in human history. We demand more and more from the earth and encourage other countries do the same. At the same time, we hold to the belief that, as a nation, we are becoming more conservative. This presents a puzzling question: Is it possible that we have changed the definition of what it means to be conservative? The words *conservative* and *conservation* share the same etymological root. Given the extremes of our materialistic culture, it is doubtful that Will Rogers would think of our contemporary society as conservative.

Will boarding airplane on Drought Relief Tour, El Paso, Texas

CONSERVATION

"We are going at top speed, because we are using all our Natural Resources up just as fast as we can. If we want to build something out of wood, all we got to do is go cut down a tree and build it. We didn't have to plant the tree. Nature did that before we come. Suppose we couldn't build something out of wood till we found a tree that we had purposely planted for that use. Say, we never would get it built. If we want anything made from steam, all we do is go dig up the coal and make the steam. Suppose we didn't have any coal and had to ship it in. If we need any more Gold or Silver, we go out and dig it; want any oil, bore a well and get some. We are certainly setting pretty right now. But when our resources run out, if we can still be ahead of other nations, then will be the time to brag; then we can show whether we are really superior.

"The Lord has sure been good to us. And what are we doing to warrant that good luck any more than any other Nation?

"And just how long is that going to last? Our good fortune can't possibly last any longer than our Natural resources.

"It just ain't in the book for us to have the best of everything all the time. We got too big an over-balance of everything and we better kinder start looking ahead and sorter taking stock and seeing where we are headed for.

"You know, I think we put too much emphasis on our so-called High standard of living. I think that 'high' is the only word in that phrase that is really correct. We sure are a-living High.

"Our Children are delivered to the schools in

Automobiles. But whether that adds to their grades is doubtful. There hasn't been a Thomas Jefferson produced in this country since we formed our first Trust. Rail splitting produced an immortal President in Abraham Lincoln; but Golf, with 20 thousand courses, hasn't produced even a good A Number-1 Congressman. There hasn't been a Patrick Henry showed up since business men quit eating lunch with their families. Suppose Teddy [Roosevelt] had took up Putting instead of horseback riding. But it ain't my business to do you folks' worrying for you. I am only tipping you off and you-all are supposed to act on it."[11]

12

SO-CALLED PROGRESS

"America invents everything, but the trouble is we get tired of it the minute the new is wore off."[1]

Will, like all of us, had a split personality when it came to progress. On the one hand, he loved the promise of all the new developments of his day. Near the end of his life he said, *"We are living in great times. A fellow can't afford to die now with all this excitement going on."*[2]

On the other hand, he could see that there was a downside to such rapid progress and he longed for simpler times,

"People take themselves too serious, they think if they don't break their neck gettin' from one place of business to another that the World will stop. Say, all they have to do is just watch some man die that is more prominent than they are, and in less than 24 hours the world has forgot he ever lived. So they ought to have imagination enough to know how long they will stop things if they left this old earth. People nowadays are traveling faster, but they are not getting any further (in fact not as far) as our old dads did."[3]

Regarding the Chicago World's Fair in 1933, Will questioned its theme, "A Century of Progress," when he pointed out, *"We were on the gold standard in 1833; there was no golf except in Scotland; there were no chamber of commerce luncheon speakers; and you lived until you died and not until you were run over by an automobile."*[4]

Although automobiles were fast becoming symbols of a newfound freedom, Will was not very fond of them. He was slow to warm up to telephones as well. But he had a romance with aviation that made him one of its biggest boosters. Ironically, this passion would lead to his death in 1935. But like so many others, Will saw airplanes, along with those who flew them, as the epitome of all that was exciting and adventurous. Defending aviation and gouging Prohibition, Will said, *"Seven people were killed in the whole of America over the weekend in airplanes, and the way the newspapers headlined it you would have thought Nicaragua had invaded us. Yet in New York City alone, fifteen was killed and seventy wounded with bad liquor, to say nothing about Chicago. So it's safer to take a flight than a drink."*[5]

Will's love of aviation combined with his general contempt for automobiles parallels our ambivalence about progress. The difference is that in Will's day, simpler times were not such a distant memory. Today we have gone so far down the technological highway that getting off now would be like trying to back down a Los Angeles freeway exit ramp. We are just too dependent on our technology to escape it.

AIRPLANES

"You haven't seen a Policeman walking on the Sidewalk since Henry Ford perfected his first Carburetor. Now that is what they call changing with the times, or Modern Progress. Everything must change. If a thing used to be good, now it must be bad. They tell you we are living in a fast age. Well, we are—IF we can live.[6]

"Here is something that we all read in the papers every morning of our lives, no matter what paper it is we pick up.

"'Four Killed and Three Wounded Yesterday by Automobiles in This Town.' Maybe it's more; maybe it's less, but it's there every day. Now right over in the adjoining column of the same edition of the paper is the following: 'Annual Auto bill of U. S. is 14 Billions of dollars per year.' That's billions, not millions, and it takes a smarter fellow than I am to even tell how many millions there is in ONE billion. In another part of the paper it tells that 22 thousand met their death last year by Auto and that we are well on our way to beat that record. Fourteen billion dollars we paid to kill 22 thousand. About $635,000 a piece, with no charge at all for the wounded. They will run at least two or three times as many as the killed, and FOR WHAT? Why, just to get somewhere a little quicker, that is if you get there at all.

"Why don't we get in an Airship? We can get there three or four times as quick as an Automobile. No Detours. No kicking about bad roads. But no, we won't do that. We haven't got the nerve. Our Alibi is, 'Well they haven't perfected them yet. They will be all right in a few years. There is a lot of improvements to make in them yet.' That's the old excuse. Aeroplanes are twice as safe now as Automobiles. It don't take any nerve to step into a fast car and go burning 'em up and down the road. But when you step off the ground and into an Aeroplane the Driver says: 'If you want speed I will show you some. There is nobody we will hit. Nothing we will run into. We got a good Ship and a wide open sky. Step in. I will shoot you out to Chicago in six hours.'

"Oh no. You want to burn up the Boulevard, but you haven't got the nerve to step in that aeroplane, where if

anything happens it ain't going to happen to anybody but you and the pilot. The pilot is willing. He knows his business. Why, the Public ain't waiting for Airships to get safer. The Public is just waiting till they can accumulate themselves some more nerve.[7]

Lance Brown and wife, Debra, flying in Alaska

"No, sir, air is the thing—get people used to getting up into it. The next war is going to be all in the air. Nobody ain't going to hand you a pair of putties and a Helmet in the next war. They are going to slip a throttle of an airship into your hands and say, 'Go aloft and see if you are lucky enough to come down of your own accord or will somebody have to bring you down.' It will be as big a disgrace ten years from now not to know how to run an airship as it is now not to know how to run a flivver.

"So if either party wants an issue that you won't have

to be ashamed of, or stand astraddle of, why, shout Airships!"[8]

It almost seems like Will is daring the public to take up flying. But he had a point. Even back when airplanes were comparatively primitive, they still had a better safety record than automobiles. And today, the number of safely flown passenger miles logged by private and commercial airplanes makes the safety record on our highways look ridiculous by comparison. But there is nothing like an airplane crash for grabbing headlines. It shocks us with the number of people lost in one incident. We think of how helpless the passengers were to do anything about their fate. Sitting behind the wheel of an automobile, we think we are more in control of our destinies. Statistics show that this is somewhat of an illusion. Because we see our cars as necessary commodities, we tend to become numb to their dangers.

AUTOMOBILES

"Now they call all these accidents PROGRESS. Well maybe it is Progress. But I tell you it certainly comes high priced. Suppose around 25 years ago when Automobiles were first invented, that a man, we will say it was Thomas A. Edison, had gone to our Government, and he had put this proposition up to them: 'I can in 25 years time have every person in America riding quickly from here to there. You will save all this slow travel of horse and buggy. Shall I go ahead with it?' 'Why sure, Mr. Edison, if you can accomplish that wonderful thing, why we, the Government are heartily in accord and sympathy with you.'

"'But,' says Mr. Edison, 'I want you to understand it fully, in order to accomplish it and when it is in operation

it will kill 15 to 20 thousand a year of your women and children and men.'

"'What! You want us to endorse some fiendish invention that will be the means of taking human life! Why you insult us by asking us to listen to such a plan! Why, if it wasn't for our previous regard for you we would have you thrown into an Asylum. How dare you talk of manufacturing something that will kill more people than a war? Why, we would rather walk from one place to another the rest of our lives than be the means of taking one single child's life.'

"If Cholera or Smallpox or some disease killed and left affected that many, why Congress and every agency of the Government would be working and appropriating money and doing every mortal thing necessary to do something about it. But as it is, we go right on. Build 'em faster and get better roads. So we can go faster and knock over more of them. This is the age of Progress.[9]

"So, you see, machinery is just doing fine. If it can't kill you, it will put you out of work.[10] *Live fast and die quick. That's the Slogan. The Humane side of anything can't compare with PROGRESS.*[11] *Monday morning after a beautiful, sunshiny Sunday finds the Undertaker singing at his work."*[12]

Although Will used strong language to make his point, he didn't place all the blame for the ills of progress on any particular individual. It was clear to him that the fault lies in human nature. We are never satisfied. When a need is presented, it is only natural that someone will find a way to fill it.

MR. FORD

"I want my friends in the Automobile business to know that I have no personal feelings against them in this suggestion. Take for instance Henry Ford. You could take every nickel he had and make him start broke in some other business tomorrow, and in 10 years he would be manufacturing nine-tenths of the World's supply of bath tubs, or own eight-tenths of the Hot Dog stands in this Country. My plan wouldn't discommode him in the least.[13]

Henry Ford and Will Rogers

"Brigham Young originated mass production, but Henry Ford was the guy that improved on it.[14] *He has had more influence on the lives and habits of this nation than any man ever produced in it. Great educators try to teach people, great preachers try to change people, but no man, produced through the accepted channels, has*

moved the world like Henry Ford. He put wheels on our homes, a man's castle is his sedan. Life's greatest catastrophe is a puncture. Americans don't fear the Lord as much as they do the next payment. Everybody is rushing to get somewhere, where they have no business, so they can hurry back to the place where they should never have left.

"So good luck, Mr. Ford. It will take a hundred years to tell whether you have helped us or hurt us, but you certainly didn't leave us like you found us."[15]

America in the 1920s was a lesson in contradictions. With the criminality spawned by Prohibition on one hand, religious zealots on the other, and people touting the virtues of fast living, easy money, and unlimited opportunity somewhere in between, the whole idea of America preaching its gospel of progress to the rest of the world struck Will as ironic. We were then, as we are now, the wealthiest country in the world, but not necessarily the happiest. One wonders what Will would think of today's shrinking world. Is it "progress" when the youth of many countries abandon their traditional ways to take on the trappings of western consumer societies? Is it healthy to promote the idea that everyone should live like Americans do?

GOSPEL OF PROGRESS

"England made 'em [China] *mad enough, but when we started in with our missionaries, that was the last straw. Imagine, with all of our crime and all of our immorality in the papers, and our small amount of attendance in our churches. Imagine their reaction to us going over there and telling them how they should live. Here we are, a nation that no one person in it ever did any job*

a month that he wasn't trying to get out of it and into something else. About as much contentment and repose as a fresh caged hyena. Then we go to tell some calm, contented people how to live.

"Why don't we go out here and tell everybody they got to smoke cigarettes and do the 'Black Bottom.' Lots of us don't like those things because we have never tried 'em and we don't care to. That's China. They have never tried our so-called progress, they like their way; it may not be the best way, but it's their way. Here is the difference between China and these other countries like us and France and England—China knows that their government will be existing, that they will be living the same 1,000 years from now as they are today. There is not a person in Europe or America that knows or even has any idea what us or our children or our nation will be twenty-five years from now. Then we call them 'heathens.'

"To us, progress is to work our way up to a 6-cylinder Buick, have a dinner jacket, belong to six luncheon clubs, and wear knee breeches on Sunday. Then go out and tell the world how the standard of living has raised. And start in telling the whole world, 'We are the only one with the right idea.'

"We and England are going to get a kick in the pants some day if we don't come home and start tending to our own business and let other people live as they want to.

"What degree of egotism is it that makes a nation or a religious organization think theirs is the very thing for the Chinese or the Zulus? Why, we can't even Christianize our Legislators!"[16]

13

CIVILIZATION—PRO AND CON

Presumably, the foundation of any civilized society rests on education. Some would say religion—others philosophy. All three will be addressed in this chapter.

In February of 1995, I had the honor of addressing the Association of Community College Trustees in Washington, DC. The Republicans had just swept the elections in '94 and were hot after their "Contract with America." The trustees had come to Washington to see whether they could talk Congress out of taking the contract out on them. After a day on the Hill, they were in need of some cheering up, and that's where Will and I came in.

EDUCATION

"You know, I am practically world famous for my ignorance.[1] *But then again, as I've always said, everybody is ignorant, only on different subjects.*[2] *Actually, the fourth reader is as far as I ever got in schools. I am not braggin' on it. I am thoroughly ashamed of it for I had every opportunity.*[3]

"First I went to Drumgoul. It was a little one-room log cabin, four miles west of Chelsea. We graduated when we could print our full name and numerate to the teacher the Nationality of the last Democratic President.[4] *After that I attended Harrell Institute, which was a girls school. Me and the president's son were the only boys there. We were*

ten years old.[5] *Then there was the Willie Halsell School. I went there awhile, in fact quite a while. I was in Ray's arithmetic three years and couldn't get to fractions. Well, I saw they wasn't running that school right. I could have taken it and made something out of it, so I just got out. That's the way I have always done with schools; the minute mine and their plans didn't jibe why I would get out, or sometimes they would ask me. I would generally always do it if they did; I was an accommodating boy.*[6]

"Then it was Kemper Military School. Kemper was not being run in accordance with the standards that I thought befitting a growing intellect. I was gonna spend my third year in the fourth grade and I wasn't being appreciated, so I not only left them flat during a dark night, but I left the entire school business for life."[7]

When Will talked about his own education, he made it appear that he had gotten very little. But even though he was the class clown and only did well in the subjects he was interested in, his education went further than he liked to admit. He would pretend to have gone through only the fourth grade, while actually he went through the tenth. He acted as if he was lazy about seeking knowledge when, in fact, he had an avid interest in history and current events. Obviously, he was bright and very well informed, with a strong memory and an insatiable curiosity. No doubt it was this curiosity that led him to be a world traveler while many of his peers stayed closer to home. The more Will saw of the world and humanity, the more he loved both. Had he stayed in school, he might have become more cynical. Instead, he acquired a broad experience and common-sense outlook that produced a unique perspective on life. He said, *"My humor is not so hot, my philosophy don't philo and my jokes are pre-war, but my good feeling toward mankind is 100 per cent."*[8]

Will could certainly give a good ration of grief to academics. But at heart, he admired educated people. If they had done the hard work necessary to educate themselves, he gave them their due. When at the height of his career, several colleges wanted to confer honorary degrees upon him, he showed his respect for what it took to get a good education by writing,

> *"Degrees have lost prestige enough as it is without handing 'em around to second-hand comedians. And its this handing 'em out too promiscuously that has helped to cheapen 'em. Let a guy get in there and battle for four years if he wants one, and don't give him one just because he happens to hold a good job in Washington, or manufactures more monkey-wrenches than anybody else or because he might be fool enough to make people laugh.*
>
> *"Keep 'em for those kids that have worked hard for 'em. Keep 'em believing in 'em. They are stepping out in the world with nothing but that sheet of paper. That's all they got. Our civilization don't offer 'em anything else. We offer him nothing. He steps into a world not of his making, so lets at least don't belittle his badge."*[9]

A high-powered education is fine but it doesn't prevent you from making mistakes. After all, even the brightest of the bright don't get it right all of the time. Albert Einstein once commented that the greatest thing about all the new technology and labor-saving devices of his day was the fact that they would free us all to study math, science, music, and art—to improve ourselves. Dr. Einstein apparently hadn't anticipated daytime television. Will summed up this kind of miscalculation pretty well when he said, "*There is nothing as stupid as an educated man if you get him off the thing he was educated in.*"[10]

The college professors and trustees were warming up to Will pretty well by now, so I let him elaborate further on their particular brand of "applesauce."

> *"Now, all of our disgustingly rich men are at a loss to know what to do with their money. Funny none of them ever thought of giving it back to the people they got it from. Instead of these men giving money to found colleges to promote learning, why don't they pass a constitutional amendment prohibiting anybody from learning anything? And if it works as good as the Prohibition one did, in five years we would have the smartest race of people on earth.*[11]
>
> *"Now take robbing. Robbing is one profession that certainly has advanced in this country. No schools or anything to learn you to rob. No other line, outside of drinking can show the progress that robbing has in the last five years. We spend billions of dollars on education and we are no smarter today than thirty years ago, and we spend nothing to foster robbing, and here it is one of the most skilled industries we have. So it sometimes makes you think what's the use of learning people anything anyway. Let 'em alone, and they will progress quicker.*[12]
>
> *"See, I believe the Lord split knowledge up among his subjects about equal after all. The so-called ignorant is happy. Maybe he is happy because he knows enough to be happy. The smart one knows he knows a lot, and that makes him unhappy because he cant impart it to all his friends. Discontent comes in proportion to knowledge.*

The more you know the more you realize you don't know.[13] *It could almost make you a democrat. 'Cause you see, dissatisfaction is what makes you a Democrat; it's not 'environment' or 'training' or 'education' really. In fact the more education you get the less apt you are to be a Democrat, and if you are very highly educated you will see the applesauce in both parties.*[14]

"Now, education never helped morals. The most savage people we have are the most moral. The smarter the guy, the bigger the rascal.[15] *I'll tell ya, villains are getting as thick as college degrees and sometimes on the same fellow.*[16]

"Besides, this bein' educated is highly overrated. These scientists can tell you just to the minute when something is going to happen ten million miles away but none of them has ever been smart enough to tell you what day to put on your heavy underwear.[17] *Some guy invented 'Vitamin A' out of a carrot. But I'll bet he cant invent a good meal out of one.*[18]

"But you know, I am strong for a good education. It will take you a long way sometimes. Take our president, Mr. Hoover. He went to Stanford University. But I tell ya, things were educationally queer in those days. Why, they even had reading and writing and Arithmetic, instead of Football, that's how primitive Stanford was. Didn't even have as much as a Golf Course. They built a Library before they built a Swimming pool. Wouldn't that make you laugh now![19]

"It's open field running that gets your old College somewhere these days and not a pack of spectacled Orators, or a mess of Civil Engineers. It's better to turn out one good Coach then Ten College Presidents. His name will be in the papers every day and it will always

be referred to where he came from. But with College Presidents, why as far as publicity is concerned, they just as well might have matriculated in Hong Kong.[20]

"But you know, they've got a pretty good 'gag' goin' in these colleges now. They slip up behind an old boy or girl and say, 'What are you going to major in?'

"'Oh, Professor, I am not going in the army. I ain't gonna to do any majoring.'

"'I mean, what is to be your life's work? Hurry up now. Let me know before noon.'

"Now, there is nothing they can do, yet they are told to make up their minds what it is. Suppose professors and teachers were told they couldn't teach any more, but to make up their minds what they were going to 'major' in? If somebody took my little jokes and good looks away from me, I know it would take me a right smart spell before I could make up my mind what to 'major' in, especially if this Eighteenth Amendment is voted out.[21]

"Well, anyway, I don't know what this is all about. 'Cause really, all this kind of 'nut' thinking is not my business anyhow. I am not going to try and muscle in on some thinker's racket.[22] *But for me, I have found that a man only learns by two things; one is reading and the other is association with smarter people. I don't like to read,*[23] *but luckily, I don't have any trouble findin' people who are smarter than I am."**

Today, we get our daily dose of murder and mayhem through a television set, but in Will's day, people got most of their information from the newspapers. Will's column, carried in over five hundred papers nationwide, became one of his best vehicles for reaching the people. It offered more than just sound bites. Will was able to discuss various subjects in considerable depth. His famous quote, *"All I know is just what I read in the newspapers"*[25] was deceptively simple. It turns out he knew quite a lot.

Will keeping current on the movie lot

CIVILIZATION

"You know, I doubt very much if Civilization (so called) helped generosity. I bet the old cave man would divide his raw meat with you as quick as one of us will ask a 'down and outer' to go in and have a meal with us. Those old boys or girls would rip off a wolf skin breech cloth and give you half of it quicker than a Ph.D. would slip you his umbrella. In those days people fought for food and in self defense. Nowadays we have diplomats work on

wars for years before arranging them. That's so that when it's over, nobody will know what they were fighting for.[26]

"But we do love to fight. It would be really wonderful if people would quit fighting. It would. But you can't blame anybody, mind you. It's just the way we are bred, that's all. If we see anything we want, we take it. The more so-called civilized we get the more we kill and take.[27] *Why, civilization is nothing but acquiring comforts for ourselves.*[28] *Here we are. The difference between our rich and poor grows greater every year. Our distribution of wealth is getting more uneven all the time.*[29] *That's because, there ain't no civilization where there ain't no satisfaction and that's what's the trouble now. Nobody is satisfied.*[30]

"No, our Civilization is not so hot.[31] *I'll tell you the truth folks, we will never have true civilization until we have learned to recognize the rights of others."*[32]

RELIGION

Jim Rogers once told me, "My father was the most religious man I ever knew. But he never preached to anyone. He just believed in living by example."

Will didn't belong to any particular church but he did countless benefits for churches and other worthy causes. While donating his time, he never asked who the needy people were, their color or their denomination. He just did the work. But he did have one little rule. He didn't believe in working on Sundays.

On one occasion, Will was asked to do a series of radio programs to be aired on Sunday nights. He kept refusing until the network finally offered him $50,000 to do the shows. (This was in the middle of the Depression, when you could buy a steak dinner for a buck.) Will did the work but he never saw a nickel of the salary. He split the money between his two favorite charities: The American Red Cross and The Salvation Army. Will didn't believe in working on Sundays – at least not for his own benefit. Dr. Reba Collins once told me that in tracing Will's career all the way back into his vaudeville days, she found that the proceeds from his Sunday performances always went to charity.

Will's charitable contributions came from both the pocketbook and the heart. When called upon, he opened both to those in need. He didn't just tolerate people, he accepted them. If there was any time when Will employed the motto, "Live and let live," it was when he discussed religion.

> *"As for me, I was raised predominantly a Methodist, but I have traveled so much, mixed with so many people in all parts of the world, I don't know just what I am. I know I have never been a non-believer. But I can honestly tell you that I don't think that any one religion is the religion. If I am broadminded in any way, and I hope I am in many, I am broadminded in a religious way. Which way you serve God will never get one word of argument or condemnation out of me.*[33]
>
> *"Why, I have worked at affairs for every denomination in the World here in New York, because one is just as worthy as the other. Old New York, the so-called heartless city, houses some great people in every denomination in the world, and I can't see any difference in them. I haven't been able to see where one has the monopoly on the right course to Heaven.*[34]
>
> *"Why, our Savior performed some pretty handy feats in the early days and his exploits have been handed down through the ages and made him our greatest hero, all accomplished without the aid of a newspaper.*[35] *But can*

you imagine our Savior dying for all of us, yet we have to argue over just whether he didn't die for us personally, and not for you? Sometimes you wonder if His lessons of sacrifice and devotion was pretty near lost on a lot of us.[36] *If some of those birds* [those arguing religion] *would spend their time following His example instead of trying to figure out His mode of arrival and departure, they would come nearer getting confidence in their church. There is no argument in the world carries the hatred that a religious belief one does and it seems the more learned a man is, the less consideration he has for another man's belief.*

"Now see, I don't happen to believe that Noah took a pair of every kind of animals into the Ark. Why I have seen men, since Prohibition changed their drink, claim that they saw animals that Noah never even heard of. But just because I don't believe Noah's African adventure, maybe others do. Besides with my small experience with animals I don't believe Noah could round up all the animals in one herd without the skunk causing a stampede. But, that is no reason why I should go around shouting about it, and be arrested for heresay. I can enjoy a good zoo as well as any one. Whether the animals come here by ark or by subway makes no difference to me. If they are going to argue religion in the church instead of teaching it, no wonder you can see more people at a circus than at a church.[37]

"If the Lord had wanted us to know exactly how, and where, and when we come, he would have let us know in the first place. He didn't leave any room for doubt when he told you how you should act when you got here. His example, and the Commandments are plain enough, so just start from there, never mind going back any farther.[38] *The Lord put all these millions of people over the earth. They don't all agree on how they got here, and ninety per*

cent don't care. But he was pretty wise when he did see to it that they all do agree on one thing (whether Christian, Heathen, or Mohammedan) and that is that the better lives you live the better you will finish."[39]

There is a lot of talk about values these days. Politicians have overused the word to the point of rendering it meaningless. When people start talking about values, we automatically brace ourselves for a self-righteous lecture that is long on mythology and short on facts. We constantly hear about our "lost values." But if Will were here, he would probably bring some balance to this subject. Will strongly believed that human nature doesn't change very much. Dishonesty, indecency, and immorality have always been with us. There were thieves, murderers, and con artists back in Will's day, just as there are now. Our past is strewn with political scandal, domestic violence, and even gang warfare. Will's society was one in which the amount of opportunity, education, or social justice you received often depended on your station in life, your race, or your religion. Things have changed a little since then, but what lies at the core of these prejudices still persists. As Will once said about some people trying to negotiate disarmament, *"The conference is off to a flying start. There is nothing to prevent their succeeding now but human nature."* [40]

But rather than give up on humanity, Will was a realist. He would probably remind us that our so-called lost values are not lost at all. The things that are noble in human beings have coexisted alongside our darker natures ever since man threw his first rock. However, to prevail, these values must be nurtured. They need constant renewal. Throughout history, our great leaders, teachers, artists, religious figures, and storytellers have had to remind us of our higher purpose.

Will Rogers, just by being his natural self at the right time in history, unintentionally filled that role. When it came to religion, he called on us to lay down our differences, seek understanding, and accept each other's beliefs.

> *"Preachers all over are telling us that there is a gradual weaning away from the church. Well, I have sometimes wondered if the preachers themselves have not something to do with this. You hear or read a sermon nowadays, and the biggest part of it is taken up by knocking or trying to prove the falseness of some other denomination. They say that the Catholics are damned, that the Jews' religion is all wrong, or that the Christian Scientists are a fake, or that the Protestants are all out of step.*
>
> *"Now, just suppose, for a change they preach to you about the Lord and not about the other fellow's church, for every man's religion is good. There is none of it bad. We are all trying to arrive at the same place according to our own conscience and teachings. It don't matter which road you take. Suppose you heard a preacher say: 'I don't care if you join my church or the other fellow's across the street. I don't claim mine to be better or worse than any other. But get with somebody and try and do better.' Hunt out and talk about the good that is in the other fellow's church, not the bad, and you will do away with all this religious hatred you hear so much of nowadays.*[41]
>
> *"It's just that there has been times when I wished there had been as much real religion among some of our creeds as there has been vanity, but that's not in any way a criticism."*[42]

PHILOSOPHY

One of Will's most famous quotes is "I never met a man I didn't like." This is also one of his most misunderstood. Many people think that Will meant to say that he liked absolutely everybody no matter what they did. But when we look at his words and attitudes throughout his life, it seems to me that he simply meant that upon meeting you, he liked you, regardless of your station in life, ethnic background, religious beliefs, or race. In other words, at a time when segregation was legal and anti-Semitism commonplace, Will stood out for being non-judgmental. I am not the first to note the profundity of this little statement. Shortly after Will's death, his friend O. O. McIntyre wrote: "If Will Rogers were not one of the most talented men of his time, he could have achieved greatness for this simple statement in a world swollen and angrily red with hate: 'I never met a man I didn't like.'"[43]

Will's compassion came from an old Indian saying, "Never judge a man until you've walked a day in his moccasins." He thought that if you stood in another person's position, understood the person's experience and motivation, you could find something of value in just about everyone. He believed this and he lived by it. Coincidentally, hardly anyone ever disappointed him. Will's simple statement, "I never met a man I didn't like," seems to be his answer to the most difficult challenge forwarded by all the world's great religions: the challenge to understand and care for our fellow travelers in this life.

This is not to say that Will was perfect. He was human, after all. Perhaps he was a bit selfish in pursuit of his career. He loved freedom and he did what he wanted to do most of the time. A less understanding family might have resented Will's restless agenda. He had a deep rooted desire to be liked – not only to be accepted, but to be praised. This is common to all of us, but especially true of entertainers. As children, we all love singing, dancing, drawing pictures, and making believe. But as we grow older, society conditions such overt behaviors out of most of us. Our natural creativity as children gets slowly whittled away by a subliminal message that tells us that spontaneity and seeking approval are off limits to adults. But people who are destined to "never grow up" find other ways of holding the limelight.

Although this attention-seeking is what initially motivates many of us to go into the arts, a mature artist balances the quest for approval with a pure love of the creative process. The applause is nice, but it eventually becomes secondary to the joy of inspired activity. This was the case with Will. As a youth, he was a cut-up in school. As an adult, Will loved his work and integrated it completely into his life. His public persona was not much different from his true self. He was no hypocrite. He sincerely liked people, he wanted them to like him, and he let it show. This often left him vulnerable. There would be times when people would openly disagree with him. They might get personal in their criticism of his viewpoint. In his column, Will would sometimes give lengthy rebuttals in which it was fairly obvious that – like a rejected child – his feelings had been hurt.

But, to err on the side of trying to be a good person, likable to all, can hardly be considered a terrible flaw. Look at the results of Will's efforts to live an exemplary life. He was a voice of reason and compassion in a time that was ripe for violence. He lifted spirits and promoted harmony in a nation stymied by the Great Depression. He traveled the country, giving material and spiritual aid that relieved the suffering of people hit with a depth of poverty that some of us can't even imagine today. The scores of anonymous contributions he made to organizations and individuals alike continue to surface even to this day. These were not given with an eye toward gaining approval. It just seems that Will Rogers was a naturally good-hearted man. I once asked Will Rogers, Jr. whether his father ever displayed a temper. He said, "Yes, he would get very angry if someone abused an animal or talked down to another person."

Lance Brown and Will Rogers, Jr.

"This week I got some interesting letters. One I sure was surprised to get was from Will Durant, a man that has studied Philosophy like Mr. Coolidge has Politics. He wanted me to write him and give him my version of 'What your Philosophy of life is?' He said, 'I who have

lived philosophy for many years turn now from it back to life itself, and ask you, as one who has lived, to give me your version. Perhaps the version of those who have lived is different from those who have merely thought.'

"A copy of this letter is being sent to Hoover, McDonald, Lloyd George, Mussolini, Marconi, Ghandi, Stalin, Trotsky, Tagore, Einstein, Edison, Ford, Eugene O'Neil, and Bernard Shaw, and three or four others. Now I don't know if this guy Durant is kidding me or not. If I got this kind of a letter from some body less I would say it's a lot of 'Hooey' and wouldn't even finish reading it. But putting me in there with that class, why I figured I better start looking into this Philosophy thing.

"I think what he is trying to get at in plain words, (leaving all the Philosophy out) is just how much better off, after all, is a highly educated man, than a dumb one? So that's how I figure is the way I got in that list. He knew that I was just as happy and contented as if I knew something, and he wanted to get the 'Dumb' angle, as well as the highbrow.

"But I can't tell this doggone Durant anything. What all of us know put together don't mean anything. Nothing don't mean anything. We are just here for a spell and pass on. Any man that thinks that Civilization has advanced is an egotist. Fords and bathtubs have moved you and cleaned you, but you was just as ignorant when you got there. We know lots of things we used to didn't know but we don't know any way to prevent 'em happening. Confucius perspired out more knowledge than the U. S. Senate has vocalized out in the last 50 years.

"We have got more tooth paste on the market, and more misery in our Courts than at any time in our existence. There ain't nothing to life but satisfaction. If you

want to ship off fat beef cattle at the end of their existence, you got to have 'em satisfied on the range. Indians and primitive races were the highest civilized, because they were more satisfied, and they depended less on each other, and took less from each other. We couldn't live a day without depending on everybody. So our civilization has given us no Liberty or Independence. Suppose the other Guy quits feeding us.

"So you see, the whole thing is a 'Racket,' so get a few laughs, do the best you can, take nothing serious, for nothing is certainly depending on this generation. Each one lives in spite of the previous one and not because of it. And don't start 'seeking knowledge' for the more you seek the nearer the 'Booby Hatch' you get.

"And don't have an ideal to work for. That's like riding towards a Mirage of a lake. When you get there it ain't there. Believe in something for another World, but don't be too set on what it is, and then you won't start out that life with a disappointment. Live your life so that whenever you lose, you are ahead."[44]

Physician/philosopher Deepak Chopra said, "Give up your rigid attachment to a specific result and live in the wisdom of uncertainty."[45] Will put it this way, "*My plan is 'Don't Plan.' Whatever you do, don't do it perfectly; live haphazard.*" [46] Will lived life one day to the next, moment to moment. On many of his journeys he would leave his tickets open-ended. That way, at the last minute, he could make little side trips to places that fascinated him. Betty would often be surprised to have Will call or write from some destination totally different from what she had expected. This random way of living was an integral part of Will's way of life, and it influenced his thinking.

Although Will was a philosopher, he did not get his philosophy from books. He got it from his life experience, his love of people, and his deep understanding of who he was. Wisdom has been defined as seeing how things are, seeing where you fit into how things are, and being joyous in that understanding. By this definition, a wise person must have a broad view of life and a lively sense of humor. This was Will Rogers. Although fully aware of the terrible extremes of the human condition, having seen firsthand some of the world's most bitter examples of ignorance, cruelty, and degradation, Will maintained a lightness of spirit and a compassion for others. He knew that you can make some things happen for yourself, but he also knew that life includes pies in the face and tripping over one's own shoelaces. Natural and spontaneous in both his words and actions, Will told us to "go with the flow" long before it became a popular slogan. Many philosophers talk of freedom, but Will Rogers was free.

14

WHAT WOULD WILL HAVE TO SAY ABOUT...?

People are always asking me, "What would Will Rogers have to say today?" Since circumstances change but human nature doesn't, I contend that he would say many of the same things now that he said back then. Will's comments have endured because of their universal nature. He was known for his ability to see the big picture. However, he also had an eye for the minutia of life and his comments were often charming. They remind us of the cowboy wisdom Will grew up with around the turn of the century. Therefore, in choosing quotes for this chapter, I thought it would be fun to see whether what Will had to say will stretch across the years to some of our more specific questions. Here in a loose kind of alphabetical order are a few not-so-often-quoted Rogerisms:

What would Will have to say about **actors' high salaries**?

"We are a 'get the dough' people, and our children are born in a commercial age. Why if a babe in arms can cry loud enough to get paid for it we are tickled to death. Make 'em pay for talent whether it's art, music, football, literature, radio announcing or flag pole sitting. Any actors that can draw 88,000 people in one day is worthy of their hire. Don't let Wall Street get all the gravy."[1]

What would Will have to say about **ancestry**?

"Ancestors don't mean a thing in our tribe. It's as unreliable as a political promise... You just don't know what will happen. You just have to raise 'em up till they are 22 or 23 and then start guessing. They no more take after their Father and Mother than a Congressman will take after a good example."[2]

What would Will have to say about collecting **antiques**?

"Us middle class never have to worry about having old furniture to point out to our friends. We buy it on payments and before it's paid for it's plenty antique."[3]

What would Will have to say about the **Arts**?

"About 9-10ths of the stuff going on under the guise of Art is the Banana Oil. They call it Art to get to take off the clothes. When you ain't nothing else, you are an Artist. It's the one thing you can claim to be and nobody can prove you ain't."[4]

What would Will have to say about our current national **attitude**?

"They say all children reach a 'smart aleck' age some time. Well our whole country is in that stage now. Every man, every denomination and every organization wants things their way. It's just one of those things we got to pass through, and we will look back and feel ashamed of ourselves afterwards."[5]

What would Will have to say about **automation**?

"Well, we been twenty years honoring and celebrating the inventor who could save a dollar by knocking somebody out of work, now we are paying for it. Machines are

a great thing, but if one replaces a hundred men, it don't buy anything, it don't eat anything, while the hundred men spend theirs back for food, shelter, and hundred of various commodities for them and their families."[6]

What would Will have to say about **automobile depreciation?**

"If somebody wants to do something for the automobile Public, let him invent a car that will sell second handed, one week after you bought it, for at least one fourth of what you gave for it. It just seems to totally ruin a car to have an owner drive it a few weeks."[7]

What would Will have to say about **bikinis**?

"I never expected to see the day when the girls would get sunburned in the places they do now."[8]

What would Will have to say about **buying on time**?

"Don't make the first payment on anything. First payments is what makes us think we were prosperous, and the other nineteen is what shows us we are broke."[9]

What would Will have to say about **cellular phones**?

"Passengers on a train in Canada talked by phone with London, England. That's not an invention, that's a pest. This means that you can't go anywhere without somebody saying, 'Mr. Jones, if you will step to the back end of the plane, that automobile salesman is on the phone.' There has been more talking and less said over phones than in Congress."[10]

What would Will have to say about **California**?

"Everything is in California, all the great sights of

nature, and along with all these wonders we have out here is the World's greatest collection of freak humans on earth. We maintain more freak religions and cults than all the rest of the world combined. Just start anything out here and if it's cuckoo enough you will get followers.[11]

"California acts a good deal like a dog pound does in any town. It gets the undesirable strays off the streets. We are the human pound of America."[12]

What would Will have to say about the tone of today's **comedy**?

"I don't think I ever hurt any man's feelings by my little gags. I know I never willfully did it. When I have to do that to make a living I will quit. I may not have always said just what they would have liked me to say but they knew it was meant in good nature."[13]

What would Will have to say about **Congress**?

"Why, I saw a headline the other day…it said 'Congress Deadlocked – Can't Act.' I think that's the greatest blessing that could befall this country.[14] *This country has come to feel the same when Congress is in session as we do when the baby gets hold of a hammer. It's just a question of how much damage he can do with it before you can take it away from him."*[15]

What would Will have to say about people wanting to amend the **Constitution**?

"Now I see where there is bills up in Congress now to change the Constitution all around, elect the President in a different way and have Congress meet at a different time. It seems the men who drew up this thing years ago didn't know much and we are just now getting a bunch

of real fellows who can take that old Parchment and fix it up like it should have been all these years. It seems it's just been luck that's got us by so far. Now when they get the Constitution all fixed up they are going to start in on the 10 Commandments, just as soon as they find somebody in Washington who has read them."[16]

What would Will have to say about **corruption**?

"It's awfully hard to get people interested in corruption unless they can get some of it."[17]

What would Will have to say about **cosmetic surgery**?

"There are today in New York City more doctors removing superfluous noses, than there are dentists removing teeth. Every nose has a doctor all its own. They are landscaping noses just like flower gardens. If an architect has not drawn up a blue print of your nose you are as old fashioned as red flannel underwear. I haven't had mine charted yet, as the face gardener said it would take more than a readjusted nose to do me any good. In fact, he said my nose was about the only thing about my face that seemed to be properly laid out."[18]

What would Will have to say about **death**?

"Folks, death knows no denomination; and death draws no color line.[19] *And if you live right, death is a joke as far as fear is concerned."*[20]

What would Will have to say about **dishonesty in public officials**?

"Shrewdness in Public life all over the World is always honored, while honesty in Public Men is generally attributed to Dumbness and is seldom rewarded.[21] *Why,*

nowadays its about as big a crime to be dumb as it is dishonest."[22]

What would Will have to say about **divorce**?

"I maintain that it should cost as much to get married as it does to get divorced. Make it look like marriage is worth as much as divorce, even if it ain't. That would also make the preachers financially independent like it has the lawyers."[23]

What would Will have to say about **election fever**?

"I honestly believe there is people so excited over this election that they think the President has something to do with running this country."[24]

What would Will have to say about **experts**?

"These old boys with a pair of specs and a tablet and pencil can sit and figure out how much wheat, corn and oats can be raised each year in order to sell each bushel of it at a profit. Then along comes a guy called 'Elements.' This bird 'Elements' never went to college, he has never been called an 'expert' and he has been laying pretty low for quite awhile, but when this guy 'Elements' breaks out he can make a sucker out of more experts than anybody."[25]

What would Will have to say about **free speech**?

"These Englishmen are about the smartest white folks there is. It's one place where fascism, communism, Hitlerism or nudism will never get anywhere. They have a park here. Hyde Park, that's just built for folks that are agin something.

"Yesterday I saw it at its best. The biggest crowd in its history. The Black Shirts were holding one meeting and the Communists, 200 yards away, holding another, and

all London in between laughin' at both sides...England has solved the talking problem.[26]

"They give 'em a Hall or a Box to stand on and say, 'Sic 'em; knock everything in sight' and when they have denounced everything from Bunions to Capitalistic Bath Tubs, then they will go home, write all week on another speech for the following Sunday and you never have any trouble with them."[27]

What would Will have to say about the **French**?

Writing from Nice, Will said, *"It's pronounced neece, not nice; they have no word for nice in French."*[28]

What would Will have to say about the **good dying young**?

"Darn it, why is it the good ones are the ones that go. That's one thing about an ornery Guy, you never hear of him dying. He is into everything else but a Coffin."[29]

What would Will have to say about **government inefficiency**?

"The government has never been accused of being a business man."[30]

What would Will have to say about **government regulation of business**?

"There is men in business that don't belong in business any more than the government does and that's why the government has to go in."[31]

What would Will have to say about **horses**?

"A man that don't love a horse, there is something the matter with him."[32]

What would Will have to say about **hunting**?

"Been looking at the pictures in the papers today of some woman that killed a lot of big game in India. I wish the Humane Society would take up one thing after killing a poor dumb animal, you are not allowed to sit on it to have your picture made. That's awful humiliating to a wild animal.[33]

"Here is queer a streak in me, I am no hunting man (or fishing either) I wish I was for there must be a lot of pleasure in it, but I just don't want to be shooting at any animal, and even a fish. I haven't got the heart to pull the hook out of him."[34]

What would Will have to say about **hypocrisy**?

"We all have our particular little line of Apple Sauce for each occasion. So lets be honest with ourselves, and not take ourselves too serious, and never condemn the other fellow for doing what we are doing every day, only in a different way."[35]

What would Will have to say about **jumping to conclusions**?

"When a fellow ain't got much mind it don't take him long to make it up."[36]

What would Will have to say about **Japanese business**?

"Well, Japan won't have her world supremacy in business long. I saw a lot of golf courses being put in. That's the beginning of a nation's commercial decline. When we traded a spade for a putter that's the way we started in the red."[37]

What would Will have to say about **kids these days**?

"It's pretty tough on us but we just can't have the children do like we do. We are always drilling into them, 'When I was a Boy we didn't do that.' But we forget that we are not doing those same old things today. We changed with the times, so we can't blame the children for just joining the times, without even having to change. We are always telling 'em what we used to not do. We didn't do it because we didn't think of it. We did everything we could think of. We drove a horse and Buggy but we don't drive one now. So we just got to sit and watch 'em go, and I tell you they got to go some to keep up with us. If anyone of us had a child that we thought was as bad as we know we are we would have cause to start to worry."[38]

What would Will have to say about **Labor**?

"Great Labor Leader, Mr. [Samuel] *Gompers, has spent his life trying to keep labor from working too hard, and he has succeeded beyond his own dreams."*[39]

What would Will have to say about **learning**?

"It seems to me that you must never tell a thing. You must illustrate it. We seem to learn through the eye and not the noggin.[40] *People's minds are changed through observation and not through argument."*[41]

What would Will have to say about **liberals**?

"A liberal is a man who wants to use his own ideas on things in preference to generations who, he knows, know more than he does."[42]

What would Will have to say about **living right**?

"Just live your life so you wouldn't be ashamed to sell your family parrot to the town gossip."[43]

What would Will have to say about **liposuction**?

"Somebody ought to figure out a reducing process where you don't have to go through any hardships in the way of denying yourself anything but just slice off a chunk someplace. They take off an arm or a leg with no danger whatever, so in this plan they could remove it from spots where a diet can't generally reach it.

"If I was one of these big Surgeons that's what I would specialize in. My calling cards would read something like this, 'Drs. Moore and White, removers of protruding hips, remakers of body lines, distorted calves removed while you wait. Legs brought back within the bounds of garters. Why reduce and have it come off the wrong place? We level all bumps and you can eat a box of chocolates while we are doing it.'"[44]

What would Will have to say about all these **mergers**?

"The day of the Guy working for himself is past. We are living in an age of 'Mergers' and 'Combines.' When your business is not doing good you combine with something and sell more stock.

"The poor little fellow, he can't combine with anything but the Sheriff in case he is going broke, which he generally is. But "Big Business" merges with another that's not going good and both do 'nothing together.'"[45]

What would Will have to say about **mothers**?

"Mothers are the only race of people that speak the same tongue. A mother in Manchuria could converse with

a mother in Nebraska and never miss a word."[46]

What would Will have to say about **narrow-mindedness**?

"You can't broaden a man's vision if he wasn't born with one."[47]

What would Will have to say about life in **New York**?

"Never a day passes in New York without some innocent bystander being shot. You just stand around this town long enough, and be innocent, and somebody is going to shoot you. One day there was four shot. That's the best shooting ever done in this town. Hard to find four innocent people in New York, even if you don't stop to shoot them."[48]

What would Will have to say about **petty issues**?

"If you can start arguing over something, and get enough publicity, and keep the argument going, you can divide our nation overnight as to whether spinach or broccoli is the most nutritious. We can get hot and bothered over nothing and cool off faster than any nation in the world."[49]

What would Will have to say about our **physical condition**?

"We ride good, but we get out of wind walking to the garage."[50]

What would Will have to say about **polls**?

"Politics is a great character builder. You have to take a referendum to see what your convictions are for that day."[51]

What would Will have to say about **public opinion**?

"There is no country in the world where a person

changes from a hero to a goat, and a goat to a hero, or vice versa, as they do with us. And all through no change in them. The change is always with us. It's not our public men that you can't put your finger on. It's our public. We are the only fleas weighing over 100 pounds. We don't know what we want, but are ready to bite somebody to get it."[52]

What would Will have to say about **Senators**?

"You know, there is nothing in the World as alike as two Senators. They all look alike, think alike, and WANT alike. They are all looking for an appointment for some Guy who helped them get theirs. [53] *But ain't it funny?...most all new Senators are earnest and mean well. Then the Air of Washington gets in their Bones and they are just as bad as the rest."*[54]

What would Will have to say about **spiritualists**?

"Us ignorant people laugh at spiritualists, but when they die they go mighty peaceful and happy, which after all is about all there is to living, is to go away satisfied. Maybe they have got 'an ace in the hole' at that."[55]

What would Will have to say about **success**?

"So what constitutes a life well spent? Love and admiration from your fellow man is all anyone can ask."[56]

What would Will have to say about **tabloids**?

"Just give anything enough publicity, and we would pay admission to see folks Guillotined. [57] *Funny thing about human nature. When we ain't feeling so good ourselves, we always want to read about somebody that is worse off than we are."*[58]

What would Will have to say about **tax cuts?**

"We've got a long-sighted govm't folks. When everybody has got money, they cut taxes. When they're broke, they raise 'em."[59]

What would Will have to say about **term limits?**

"A man's thoughts are naturally on his next term, more than on his country.[60] *Elect 'em for a six-year term, not allow 'em to succeed themselves. That will keep their minds off politics."*[61]

What would Will have to say about **Thanksgiving?**

"Those old boys in the Fall of the year, if they could gather in a few pumpkins, potatoes and some corn for the winter, they was in a thanking mood. But if we can't gather in a new Buick, a new radio, a tuxedo and some government relief, why we feel like the world is agin us."[62]

What would Will have to say about **tipping?**

"I just wonder if it ain't just cowardice instead of generosity that makes us give most of our tips."[63]

What would Will have to say about **traffic?**

"I see Los Angeles has a big traffic problem. Too many cars. Not enough places to park 'em all. But I'll tell you how to solve L.A.'s traffic problem. All you have to do is take all the cars off the road that aren't paid for. That'll do it. It'll turn them boulevards into playgrounds overnight."[64]

What would Will have to say about **trickle-down economics?**

"Water goes down hill and moistens everything on its

way, but gold or money goes uphill. The Reconstruction loaned the railroads money, medium and small banks money, and all they did with it was pay off what they owed to New York banks. So the money went uphill instead of down. You can drop a bag of gold in Death Valley, which is below sea level, and before Saturday it will be home to papa J. P. [Morgan] [65]

"Give it to the people at the bottom and the people at the top will have it before night anyhow. But it will at least have passed through the poor fellow's hands."[66]

What would Will have to say about our **vanity**?

"Beauty Parlors are thicker than filling stations, but more power to the people that run 'em, for they earn it for having to listen to people with nothing on their mind but wanting to look better."[67]

What would Will have to say about **visionaries**?

"It takes years in this country to tell whether anybody's is right or wrong. It's kinder of a case of just how far ahead you can see. The fellow that can only see a week ahead is always the popular fellow, for he looking with the crowd. But the one that can see years ahead. He has a telescope but he can't make anybody believe he has it."[68]

What would Will have to say about today's tougher **viruses**?

"In the old days when we wasn't so sanitary, why we were strong enough to withstand all the germs. But nowadays we have to be careful of the Microbes for if they get a hold on us we are gone. We are not physically able to withstand 'em. In the old days as many as wanted to could drink out of one cup, and the last one would just shake his head and swallow down Mike-Robies just as fast as they

would acumilate. But now the old individual cup won't go for over one sitting, or it will knock the second individual right into the infested class. The old fashioned Goard that the whole family drank out of from birth till death, would kill off more of the modern population than a war."[69]

What would Will have to say about **voter apathy**?

"Our two national parties have got to a point where there's no difference in them anyhow. Whatever one will promise, the other will see him and then raise him. Then if there's a third party it adds up what the other two have promised and it'll promise as much as both of them combined, and the general public, I don't know, they've just lost all interest and don't care nothing about it.[70]

"It's just got so that 90 percent of the people in this country don't give a damn. Politics ain't worrying this country one tenth as much as parking space."[71]

What would Will have to say about **welfare**?

"Nobody can kick on honest deserving relief, and nobody can be blamed for kicking on relieving somebody when they won't work. The governments and towns have got to find some way of telling them apart.[72]

"If you don't work they pay you. I told them that wouldn't do. We've tried it with congress and the senate for years and it's a failure."[73]

What would Will have to say about **wider cars**?

"Now they are 'increasing the length, and the width of the body – 7 inches longer and 4 inches wider.' You know what those inches will do? How many times have you missed one by less than 4 inches? From now on you will hit 'em."[74]

What would Will have to say about **worry**?

"I wasn't worried. I was just 'confused.' There is quite a difference. When you are worried you know what you are worried about, but when you are 'confused' it's when you don't know enough about a thing to be worried."[75]

What would Will have to say about **women in politics**?

"There is no stopping these Women when they get started. Why I wouldn't be a bit surprised that it won't be no time till some Woman will become so desperate Politically and just lose all prospectus of right and wrong and maybe go from bad to worse and finally wind up in the Senate.

To us fellows that are not in Politics we are tickled to death, to see the Women folks dealing such misery to the Politicians. And in the long run it's good for humanity. Every job a Woman can grab off it just drives another Politician to either work or the poor house."[76]

What would Will have to say about **Women's Liberation**?

"I don't suppose there is any country, unless it be India, where the wife is more downtrodden than they are in the United States.

"Amelia Putnam [Earhart] *flew across the Atlantic Ocean and then had to call up her husband to see if he thought it would be safe for a married woman to venture into London alone.*

"But, by golly, us old scared males, our hats are off to Amelia. Her bravery is only surpassed by her skill. But, there is no use kidding ourselves. It does make a 'sucker' Out of us men. While the men are playing bridge and arguing over their golf scores, the women are flying the ocean."[77]

15

HEROES AND HOPE

"This thing of being a hero, about the main thing to it is to know when to die. Prolonged life has ruined more men than it ever made."[1]

Will Rogers was one of our most loved citizens. In a time of scarcity and struggle, he seemed to personify what was honest and decent about us. So much so that for years after his death, many could remember exactly where they were when they heard the news. It was August 15, 1935, and the headlines read, "Rogers & Post Dead in Crash." No one had to be told who Rogers and Post were.

Wiley Post, like Will, was an Oklahoma boy. To many, he was a symbol of heroism, ability, and nerve. A true pioneer of aviation, he broke the round-the-world speed record twice, the second time solo. He invented the high-altitude pressure suit and used it to set many world altitude records. In that process, he discovered the jet stream that we all take for granted now. As a young man, Wiley lost his left eye in an oil field accident. Undaunted by his injury, he used the insurance settlement to buy his first airplane and went on to become one of the best pilots of his day. Wiley's distinctive eye patch even gave him the look of an adventurer. Will said of Wiley, *"Wiley Post is just about king of 'em all."*[2] He described him as *"...tough as a boot physically, and as determined as a bull."*[3]

In 1935, Will was at the peak of his career: making movies, doing radio shows, writing his column, performing on stage, doing benefit work, and speaking at special occasions across the land. By summer, things were so hectic that Will was starting to burn out. A sightseeing tour of Alaska seemed like a perfect way to get away from it all. The trip was intended to be largely recreational. But it also provided a means for Will to gather material for his column. It was Will's insatiable appetite for new material that led the duo to Barrow. A renowned pioneer, Charles D. Brower, had lived above the Arctic Circle far longer than any other white man, and Will wanted to interview him.

Will Rogers and Wiley Post en route to Barrow

Thrilled to be seeing new territory, Will was intent on sharing his adventure with everyone. As the little plane streaked across the Alaskan wilderness, he used his weekly column and daily telegrams to take his readers along for the ride. He described the landscape, the people, the plane, and its pilot. Will was so taken with Wiley's brilliant red experimental airplane, with its big radial engine and long dramatic pontoons, that he sent a photograph of it home to his family. On it he wrote, "She is a Beaut, ain't it?" But that same airplane, when it lost power, became uncontrollable, and it crashed into an inlet just off the Arctic Ocean, about sixteen miles south of their final destination. Both Will and Wiley were killed instantly.

The only witnesses to the accident were a small group of Eskimos who were hunting seal near the Walakpa Lagoon. Claire Okpeaha and his wife were camped on the river bank. It was a heavily overcast day. Running low on fuel, Wiley found a break in the clouds and made a landing on the river. He brought the plane close to the shore so that Will could get out on the pontoon to ask for directions to Barrow. After Okpeaha pointed the way, Will climbed back into the plane. They taxied out into open water, revved the big engine into a deafening roar and took off. At about fifty feet, they started a banking turn to the right. The engine sputtered and stalled. A few seconds of silence preceded the crash—a hollow moment of anticipation—and then, impact! In the briefest of moments, what was once a graceful scarlet bird lay mangled in the shallow water. Okpeaha got as close to the wreck as possible and shouted. Getting no response, he turned and ran the sixteen miles to Barrow for help. Arriving exhausted, he described what he had seen.

When the rescue party arrived, they found Will in the back of the plane, his skull crushed and his legs broken. It has been speculated that, because of the apparent nose heaviness of the aircraft, Wiley would have Will climb into the tail section before take-off to provide some extra weight in the back. Will's body was easily removed, but Wiley's was

Crash scene

not. He was found pinned against a pontoon with part of his body crushed under the enormous engine. Working in the shallow water with only primitive Eskimo tools, the party struggled for hours to free Wiley from the wreckage. The arrival of a block and tackle finally did the job. Both bodies were wrapped in sleeping bags and gently placed into separate boats. Huddled against the changing weather, the party started back to Barrow.

The white men in the group were clearly traumatized by the loss of these two men. Noticing this, the Eskimos started singing an Inuit hymn that was reserved only for the time of the passing of the most powerful men in their tribe. They sang the eerie song over and over in the three hours it took to navigate the ice floe back to Barrow. When they finally beached the boats, everybody in the party was singing that song. They didn't know what the words meant but they certainly knew the sentiment.

A wire was sent down to the forty-eight states and this whole country went into shock. Businesses were closed and workers were sent home that day. There was a moment of silence on the floors of both the House and the Senate when they heard the news. Carl Sandburg said that the nation had not experienced such an outpouring of grief since the death of Lincoln. The national reaction was best summed up by an old family friend, John McCormack. He was an Irish tenor from the Ziegfeld Follies days, and he captured the mood of the nation when he paraphrased Shakespeare's Hamlet, saying, "A smile has disappeared from the lips of America, and her eyes now are suffused with tears. He was a man, take this for all in all, and we shall not look on his like again."

People felt as if they had lost a family member when they lost Will Rogers. Heads of state, religious leaders, and common folks alike poured out heartfelt eulogies in remembrance of this congenial wisecracking fellow. He was a hero to them. People had heroes in those days. It was OK to have a hero.

I cannot think of heroes without remembering a fellow who came up to me after a show one time and said, "You know, if you're a hero worshipper, I bet I could find you a psychiatrist that would tell you that you've got something wrong with your self esteem." The only way I could think to respond to such a statement was to say, "Bull!"

There is nothing wrong with having a hero – especially one like Will Rogers. We are not talking about the kind of hero worship that created a Nazi Germany here. We are simply talking about looking up to and respecting a fellow citizen who happens to be a symbol of honesty, decency, integrity – all of those things we want to teach to our children, all of those things we expect from our leaders and all of those things that we have to embody ourselves if this little experiment in democracy is going to work out all right. So why shouldn't that man be a national hero?

Daniel Boorstin, Historian, Pulitzer Prize-winning author, and former Librarian of Congress, warns, "Read history, read books, not just newspapers and magazines. The temptation to make your contemporaries into heroes is the temptation to see them as divine. That is what happened with Hitler.

"The hero is known for achievements, the celebrity for well-knownness. The hero reveals the possibilities of human nature, the celebrity reveals the possibilities of the press and the media. Celebrities are people who make the news, but heroes are people who make history. Time makes heroes but dissolves celebrities."[4]

As far as I am concerned, Will Rogers meets Mr. Boorstin's criteria for a hero. True, he was a celebrity. But he went beyond his celebrity to live an exemplary life. Will was not an athlete, a general, or a great scientist, but he was a model citizen who gave away over half of his time and half of his fortune to those less fortunate than himself. He was a major player in the moral and social fabric of his day, a voice of reason and compassion in a world ripe for conflict. He lifted the spirits of a nation burdened with economic depression and in danger of dropping into despair. He demonstrated that it was possible to rise to the top of one's chosen field of endeavor while maintaining the humility of one's origins. He made history every time he set aside his own personal gain to go on backbreaking benefit tours, helping earthquake victims in Nicaragua, flood victims along the Mississippi, or drought victims during the Dust Bowl days of the 1930s. I have experienced personally how the legacy of Will Rogers has stood the test of time and how his heroism, humor, and wisdom still resonates with us today.

In my travels, often I hear people say, "We need more heroes for our children to look up to." Heroes do seem to be in short supply these days. But in a recent poll, when asked who their heroes were, 65% of teenage respondents who had heroes pointed to one or both of their parents. Others chose teachers, coaches, and counselors – people directly involved in their lives as role models. A much smaller percentage than you would think chose celebrities.

If we asked Will Rogers, "How can we have more heroes for our children to look up to?," I could almost guarantee you that he would say the best way would be to look toward what is most heroic in ourselves. Will didn't want anyone to be like him. He was best at being himself, and he expected the same of everybody else. Unlike many of the heroes manufactured for us on our TV screens and in our movie theaters today, Will Rogers was a natural man. He was real! What you saw on the screen, what you heard on the radio, what you read in the paper—that's the way he really was: a genuine human being, living up to his full potential. Will Rogers has been aptly described as a very *uncommon*, common man.

HOPE

If Will were alive today would he be in despair about the state of our world? I think not. This is not to say there are no reasons to be anxious about the future. The media provide daily statistics that show us to be on a collision course with crime, poverty, other nations, and the environment. But during Will's day, people faced similar threats. They had experienced a great World War, economic fluctuations that eventually bottomed out in the Great Depression, technological advances that displaced workers, political scandals that eroded public confidence, and competing ideologies that threatened traditional values. But through it all, Will had an immovable faith in the average American citizen. Although he teased us for our vanities and chastised us for our excesses, at heart, he felt that the common people were the true face of America and the hope for the future.

> "*Now I am going to take up the subject* [Americanism] *and see what I can wrestle out of it. Let's*

get our rope ready and turn it out, and we will catch it and see really what brands it has on it. Here it comes out of the Corral. We got it caught; now it's throwed and Hog Tied; and we will pick the Brands and see what they are.

"The first thing I find out is there ain't any such animal. The American Animal that I thought I had here is nothing but the big Honest Majority, that you might find in any Country. He is not a Politician. He is not a 100 per cent American. He is not any organization, either uplift or downfall. In fact I find he don't belong to anything. He is of no decided Political faith or religion. I can't even find out what religious brand is on him. From his earmarks he has never made a speech, and announced that he was An American. He hasn't denounced anything. It looks to me like he is just an Animal that has been going along, believing in right, doing right, tending to his own business, letting the other fellows alone.

"He don't seem to be simple enough minded to believe that EVERYTHING is right and he don't appear to be Cuckoo enough to think that EVERYTHING is wrong. He don't seem to be a Prodigy, and he don't seem to be a Simp. In fact, all I can find out about him is that he is just NORMAL. After I let him up and get on my Horse and ride away, I look around and I see hundreds and hundreds of exactly the same marks and Brands. In fact they so far outnumber the freaky branded ones that the only conclusion I can come to is that this Normal breed is so far in the majority that there is no use to worry about the others. They are a lot of Mavericks, and Strays."[5]

Will's faith in the future also rested on his belief in the American way of life. He supported the Constitution with its system of checks and balances. Admitting that our governing process is cumbersome at best, he often praised it as a necessary evil to insure a proper balance of freedom and opportunity. Having witnessed other systems first-hand, Will fully understood how the vision of our country's founders has always thwarted tyranny on these shores. Not being one to use flowery language, Will put it this way;

> *"This country is just the same as it was, and always will be, because it is founded on right and even if everybody in public life tried to ruin it they couldn't. This country is not where it is today on account of any man. It is here on account of the big normal majority. A politician is just like a necktie salesman in a big department store. If he decides to give all the ties away, or decides to pocket all the receipts, it don't effect the store. It don't close. He closes, as soon as he is found out.*[6]
>
> *"Every time we have an election we get in worse men, and the country keeps right on going. Time has only proven one thing, and that is that you can't ruin this country even with politics."*[7]

In the period just after Will's death, many of his movies were held off the market. Twentieth Century Fox did not want to appear to be financially exploiting Will's passing, a concept foreign to our business practices today. During the Great Depression, many people drew a kind of spiritual sustenance from watching Will's movies, listening to him on the radio, and reading his column. Will harkened back to the nation's founders, the Old West, and a period of self-reliance that inspired people and gave them hope during hard times.

With the advent of World War II, much of Hollywood's energies were channeled into the war effort. As Will's pictures lost screen time, his popularity started to wane. After the war was over, all eyes were on the future. The economy was booming, people were building nest eggs, taking out FHA loans and going to school on the GI Bill. The folksy humor of Will Rogers was seen as old-fashioned and not at all in harmony with a budding consumer society. As government became a bigger player in both corporate and private life, President Eisenhower warned of a dangerous military/industrial complex. Bureaucracy flourished and kids started listening to rock and roll.

The '60s and '70s brought the Vietnam War, the Sexual Revolution, the Civil Rights Movement, and more equal participation of women and minorities in society. Will Rogers, always good for a laugh, became little more than a convenient source of pithy comments used to open speeches by politicians and after-dinner speakers.

The '80s brought about the consolidation of our consumer society, appropriately termed "McWorld." It was the decade of the car phone, the fax machine, and the power lunch. And now, as we face the millennium, we are asking ourselves, "At what price progress?"

In seeking an answer, we tend to be nostalgic about the "good old days." Most of us have in mind a 1950s "Ozzie and Harriet" version of reality that existed for relatively few people. The prosperity and stability at the close of World War II were the exception rather than the rule in American history. Whether the "good old days" were actually good depended strictly upon one's position in society. Those who did not conform to the cultural norms of the day were typically shunned. Those who were not white and/or male had to settle for limited roles in society and the crumbs of the marketplace. And who can forget the McCarthy Era with its witch hunts, blacklists, and guilt by association?

To get a better sense of the norm in America, we have to

jump back over the '50s to the time when Will Rogers lived. The period from the turn of the century to the Great Depression was, though not identical, in many ways very similar to today. There was a budding global economy, new technology was changing the nature of work, and women were demanding the vote and other rights. The criminal activities that centered around Prohibition were threatening our youth. Families were being disrupted by the work demands of new industries. There were violent clashes between demonstrating citizens and law enforcement. Race riots and labor unrest were common, and heavy immigration of largely unskilled workers fed dismal conditions in inner-city slums. While some lived a pastoral life of relative isolation in rural communities, few people today wax nostalgic about the many injustices that happened in places that were hidden from larger public scrutiny. We don't like to be reminded that lynchings occurred, and domestic violence was something best not talked about.

On balance, our situation is in many ways far better than the "good old days." Even so, we find ourselves worrying that hard times could be just around the corner. All of our modern conveniences provide little comfort as we wonder whether we might have traded some of the good things of our past for our present material affluence. We wonder whether our society has the cohesiveness to meet the challenges of another Great Depression.

But if we aren't careful, our anxiety can deceive us into thinking that the solution to our future lies in a return to the past. We all know that time is a one-way street. There is no going back – and who would want to? But, hopefully, we can glean from our ancestors some of the qualities that helped them to survive those trying times. If we can, surely we can make things better for ourselves and for those who will follow. Today's challenges are neither greater nor less than those of our predecessors—just different.

Will encouraged us to do our best and cautioned us not to get too worked up about things that were out of our control. Whatever challenges we faced as a nation, he thought it best not to count on much help from our politicians.

Will Rogers—A "Regular Bird"

"We been staggering along now about 155 years under every conceivable horse thief that could get into office, and yet here we are, still going strong. I doubt if Barnum's circus, or Hagenback's Wild Animal Circus has housed as many different kinds of species as has been in our Government employ during its existence. Yet as bad as they

are they can't spoil it, and as good as they are they can't help it. A good man can't do nothing in office because the system is against him, and a bad one can't do anything for the same reason. So as bad as we are, we are better off than any other nation, so what's the use of worry?"[8]

Will Rogers resonates with us today because he represents that part of us we would like to retrieve: the good stuff of yesterday. He knew he could not solve all of the world's problems, but he helped out whenever and wherever he was needed. Showing kindness and good humor in all of his dealings with people, Will refused to listen to those who would divide us by preaching fear and hatred. He knew that the "regular bird" was no fool and should not be sold short. By seeing through fanaticism, demagoguery, and sham, he became the spokesman for the common people of his day. He had a strong sense of community and an equally strong sense of personal responsibility. By showing us that our similarities far outweigh our differences, he left the world a better place than he found it. To Will it was all pretty simple, really: Try to live a good life, do your part to help out, and don't worry too much about the state of the nation. Things will work out in the long run.

"We are just a river flowing along. We have a drought year, and we have a flood year. They build dams to stop us, but we just fill up and flow on over 'em, so there is really nothing that can be done about us. We are just flowing to the sea. Corruption can't retard us, and reformers can't assist us, we are just flowing along in spite of everything."[9]

ACKNOWLEDGMENTS

My special thanks and heart felt gratitude go out to Debra Leyva-Brown, my wife and soul mate, for shepherding me along with patience, love, and understanding, for being a sounding board for every small point and for reading all those rough drafts. Joseph H. Carter; Director Will Rogers Memorial, Claremore, OK, for his unwavering support over the years and our shared commitment to the legacy of Will Rogers. Jim Rogers for being his natural self and giving me a sense of what it might have been like to spend some time with Will Rogers. The late Will Rogers, Jr., for letting me pick his brain about his dad when he wasn't feeling that well. Of course, Will Rogers, Sr., for his example and inspiration. Will Rogers Heritage, Inc., for developing the Interactive Multimedia CD-ROM *Presenting Will Rogers*. Pat Lowe, Librarian; Greg Malak, Curator; and the support staff of the Will Rogers Memorial, for their expert advice, research assistance, and help with the nuts and bolts of this project. Joann Murdock of Artists of Note, Inc., for keeping me working enough to meet the bills but not so much that I had no time to write. You can start responding fully to demand again. Dr. Reba Neighbors Collins, Director Emeritus Will Rogers Memorial, for sound advice in the early days, help in maintaining focus, and all of her encouragement along the way. Dr. Brian Gratton, for tough criticism that made me do a better job. I trust that if any compliments are forthcoming they will be sincere. Julie Zimmerman, for staying in touch all these years and for her generous hard work in support of this endeavor. "Wiley" Jim Pfeiffer, for lessons in the "Cowboy Way." Sue Wallis, Director Western Folklife Center, Elko, NV, for sharing her angle on the West and its people. Al and Sandy Westcott, for helpful feedback, a warm bed in St. Louis, and so many years of friendship. Rosemary Crowley, for a learned read and good input. Lillian Goldstine, for asking me to tell more about Betty Blake Rogers. Ken and Griselda Lewis, for teaching me the Texas Skip and giving me a bed and a meal every time I came through Akron. Peggy Perkins, for her experience and eye for detail. Pat Barmore, for telephone consultations on the poetry of the thing.

NOTES

Note: All quotes from daily telegrams and weekly articles are taken from *Will Rogers' Daily Telegrams*, © 1979, and *Will Rogers' Weekly Articles*, © 1980, Oklahoma State University Press as accessed through *Presenting WILL ROGERS on Interactive Multimedia CD-ROM*, © 1995, Will Rogers Memorial, P.O. Box 157, Claremore, Oklahoma 74018.

Prologue

[1]Daily Telegram, May 11, 1931.
[2]Daily Telegram, March 4, 1932.
[3]Daily Telegram, May 10, 1931.
[4]Weekly Article #90, 1924.
[5]Daily Telegram, February 28, 1930.

Introduction

[1]Weekly Article #514, 1932.
[2]*Never Met a Man I Didn't Like* by Joseph H. Carter, Avon Books, p. 62.
[3]Daily Telegram, August 2, 1932.

Chapter 1, Will Rogers—Life and Times

[1]Weekly Article #353, 1929.
[2]Weekly Article #267, 1928.
[3]Weekly Article #559, 1933.
[4]Daily Telegram, September 4, 1932.
[5]Weekly Article #119, 1925.
[6]Alex Ayers, *The Wit and Wisdom of Will Rogers*, Meridian Books, p. 88.
[7]Richard M. Ketchum, *Will Rogers – The Man and His Times*, Simon and Schuster, p.39.
[8]Joseph H. Carter, *Never Met a Man I Didn't Like*, Avon Books, p.22.
[9]Weekly Article #523, 1933.
[10]Dr. Reba Collins, *Will Rogers – Courtship and Correspondence 1900–1915*, Neighbors & Quaid, p. 178.
[11]Weekly Article #62, 1924.
[12]Weekly Article #62, 1924.
[13]Weekly Article #392, 1930.
[14]Weekly Article #59, 1934.
[15]Weekly Article #326, 1929.
[16]Will Rogers, *There's Not A Bathing Suit In Russia*, CD-ROM *Presenting Will Rogers*, Will Rogers Memorial, Claremore, Oklahoma
[17]Bryan B. & Francis N. Sterling, *A Will Rogers Treasury*, Crown Publishers, p. 5.
[18]Weekly Article #461, 1931.
[19]Daily Telegram, August 10, 1931.
[20]Radio Broadcast, Good Gulf Show, April 21, 1935.
[21]Daily Telegram, March 5, 1933.
[22]Joseph H. Carter, *Never Met a Man I Didn't Like*, Avon Books, p. 270.

Chapter 2, Bacon and Beans But No Extremes

[1]Weekly Article #470, 1931.
*In Will's time, although the term "liberal" had a political meaning, it was also used to mean "generous" or "tolerant." Since this speech is an appeal for financial help from the general public, we can assume Will would not politicize the issue. Had he intended a political meaning, he probably would have used a term like "progressive."
[3]President's Organization on Unemployment Relief Broadcast, October 18, 1931.
[4]Weekly Article #622, 1934.
[5]Daily Telegram, March 20, 1932.
[6]Weekly Article #100, 1924.

[7]Weekly Article #524, 1933.
[8]*Saturday Evening Post*, November 6, 1926.
[9]*Saturday Evening Post*, December 4, 1926.

Chapter 3, Commit the Crime, Do the Time

[1]Daily Telegram, March 11, 1932.
[2]Weekly Article #441, 1931.
[3]Daily Telegram, August 31, 1932.
[4]Daily Telegram, October 18, 1934.
[5]Daily Telegram, June 10, 1935.
[6]Daily Telegram, August 31, 1932.
[7]Weekly Article #216, 1927.
[8]Weekly Article #242, 1927.
[9]Daily Telegram, May 14, 1934.
[10]Daily Telegram, January 23, 1928.
[11]Daily Telegram, January 24, 1930.
[12]Daily Telegram, May 12, 1927.
[13]Daily Telegram, December 18, 1930.
[14]Daily Telegram, December 12, 1929.
[15]Daily Telegram, March 20, 1931.
[16]Weekly Article #145, 1925.

Chapter 4, Will's Country–Right and Wrong

[1]*Saturday Evening Post*, May 12, 1928.
[2]Daily Telegram, September 16, 1933.
[3]Daily Telegram, August 9, 1933.
[4]Daily Telegram, September 12, 1933.
[5]Daily Telegram, December 4, 1931.
[6]Daily Telegram, March 25, 1934.
[7]Daily Telegram, May 1, 1932.
[8]Daily Telegram, September 8, 1930.
[9]Weekly Article #332, 1929.
[10]Daily Telegram, June 24, 1934.
[11]Daily Telegram, December 14, 1934.
[12]Daily Telegram, February 26, 1933.
[13]Weekly Article #57, 1924.
[14]Daily Telegram, July 15, 1929.
[15]Daily Telegram, February 28, 1933.
[16]Daily Telegram, May 8, 1929.
[17]Daily Telegram, December 18, 1934.
[18]Daily Telegram, August 29, 1928.
[19]Daily Telegram, November 13, 1926.
[20]Weekly Article #26, 1923.
[21]Weekly Article #113, 1925.
[22]Daily Telegram, May 31, 1929.
[23]Daily Telegram, November 12, 1930.
[24]Weekly Article #538, 1933.
[25]Daily Telegram, February 3, 1933.
[26]Daily Telegram, April 26, 1934.
[27]Daily Telegram, March 27, 1933.
[28]Daily Telegram, February 15, 1934.
[29]Daily Telegram, November 1, 1927.
[30]Weekly Article #255, 1927.
[31]Richard M. Ketchum, *Will Rogers – The Man and His Times*, Simon and Schuster, p. 218

Chapter 5, Cannibals, Loan Sharks, and Businessmen

[1]*Los Angeles Times*, November 10, 1932.
[2]Editorial, *Chicago Tribune*, September 1, 1995.
[3]Daily Telegram, December 30, 1934.
[4]Daily Telegram, March 15, 1927.
[5]Weekly Article #48, 1923.
[6]Daily Telegram, October 12, 1930.
[7]Weekly Article #410, 1930.
[8]Weekly Article #5, 1923.
[9]Daily Telegram, June 15, 1931.
[10]Daily Telegram, July 16, 1935.
[11]Weekly Article #659, 1935.
[12]*Will Rogers, Introduction to Cowboy Philosopher on the Peace Conference*, CD-ROM *Presenting Will Rogers*, Will Rogers Memorial, Claremore, Oklahoma
[13]Will Rogers Memorial Archives Scrap Book 8-1 p. 26.
[14]Weekly Article #657, 1935.
[15]Weekly Article #129, 1925.
[16]Weekly Article #657, 1935.
[17]Bryan and Frances Sterling, *A Will Rogers Treasury*, Crown Publishers, p. 19–20.
[18]Weekly Article #217, 1927.
[19]Weekly Article #14, 1923.
[20]Richard M. Ketchum, *Will Rogers – The Man and His Times*, Simon and Schuster, p. 176–177
[21]Weekly Article #6, 1923.
[22]"How to be Funny", *American Magazine*, December 1929.
[23]Weekly Article #122, 1925.

Chapter 6, Media Magic and Modesty

[1]November 25, 1934 in Rogers, Arkansas, celebrating his 26th wedding anniversary.
[2]"Betty Blake – The Brains behind Will Rogers", Joseph H. Carter, *Ozarks This Week*, April 7, 1995.
[3]"Rogers' Leading Lady," printed by the Rogers Historical Museum, Rogers, Arkansas, 1989.
[4]E. R. Squibb & Sons Broadcast, May 11, 1930.
[5]Weekly Article #90, 1924.
[6]Richard M. Ketchum, *Will Rogers-The Man and His Times*, Simon & Schuster. p. 261 – 262.
[7]Joseph H. Carter, *Never Met a Man I Didn't Like Avon Books*, p. 62
[8]"How to be Funny," *American Magazine*, September 1929.
[9]Richard M. Ketchum, *Will Rogers – The Man and His Times*, Simon and Schuster, p. 341 – 342
[10]Radio Broadcast, Good Gulf Show, July 8, 1934.
[11]Weekly Article #601, 1934.
[12]Weekly Article #193, 1926.
[13]Weekly Article #635, 1935.
[14]Joseph H. Carter, *Never Met a Man I Didn't Like*, Avon Books, p. 96.
[15]Will Rogers Memorial Archives, *New McClures Magazine*, Sept. 1928.

Chapter 7, Will's Near-Death Experience

[1]Will Rogers, *Ether and Me* or '*Just Relax*,' CD-ROM *Presenting Will Rogers*, Will Rogers Memorial, Claremore, Oklahoma.
[2]Scott Cunningham, Our Will, (newspaper story), Chapter XVI, 1935.

Chapter 8, All That Drinkin' and Gamblin'

[1]Will Rogers, *The Cowboy Philosopher on Prohibition*, CD-ROM *Presenting Will Rogers*, Will Rogers Memorial, Claremore, Oklahoma.
[2]*Saturday Evening Post*, October 29, 1927.
[3]Radio Broadcast, E. R. Squibb & Sons, June 8, 1930.
[4]Radio Broadcast, Good Gulf Show, April 30, 1933.
[5]*Saturday Evening Post*, August 28, 1926.
[6]Weekly Article #161, 1926.
[7]Daily Telegram, October 31, 1929.

[8]Weekly Article # 361, 1929.
[9]Saturday Evening Post, February 27, 1932.
[10]Weekly Article #419, 1931.
[11]Weekly Article #461, 1931.
[12]Radio Broadcast, Good Gulf Show, May 5, 1935.
[13]Will Rogers Memorial Archives Scrap Book 8-1, p. 31
[14]Weekly Article #359, 1929.

Chapter 9, "Boodgetary" Matters

[1]Weekly Article #128, 1925.
[2]Daily Telegram, February 5, 1934.
[3]Weekly Article #483, 1932.
[4]Weekly Article #14, 1923.
[5]Daily Telegram, September 6, 1928.
[6]Daily Telegram, April 24, 1930.
[7]Weekly Article #161, 1926.
[8]Daily Telegram, February 12, 1932.
[9]Daily Telegram, March 1, 1931.
[10]Daily Telegram, February 22, 1931.
[11]Weekly Article #451, 1931.
[12]Radio Broadcast, Good Gulf Show, April 28, 1935.
[13]Radio Broadcast, Good Gulf Show, April 7, 1935.
[14]Radio Broadcast, Good Gulf Show, April 21, 1935.
[15]Radio Broadcast, Good Gulf Show, April 28, 1935.
[16]Daily Telegram, March 15, 1929.
[17]Weekly Article #97, 1924.
[18]Radio Broadcast, Good Gulf Show, June 9, 1935.
[19]Daily Telegram, February 29,1932.
[20]Daily Telegram, September 29, 1929.
[21]Weekly Article #657, 1935.
[22]Weekly Article #99, 1924.
[23]Daily Telegram, September 7, 1931.
[24]Daily Telegram, March 17, 1932.

Chapter 10, Applesauce

[1]Weekly Article #3, 1922.
[2]Daily Telegram, November 1, 1932.
[3]Radio Broadcasts, CD-ROM *Presenting Will Rogers*, Will Rogers Memorial, Claremore, Oklahoma.
[4]Daily Telegram, February 2, 1928.
[5]Weekly Article #6, 1932.
[6]Ben Yagoda, *Will Rogers – A Biography*, Knopf Publisher, p. 298.
[7]Joseph H. Carter, *Never Met a Man I Didn't Like*, Avon Books, p. 186.
[8]Paula McSpadden Love, *The Will Rogers Book*, Texian Press, p. 41.
[9]Weekly Article #470, 1931.
[10]Weekly Article #31, 1923.
[11]Daily Telegram, October 8, 1928.
[12]Daily Telegram, November 7, 1928.
[13]Weekly Article #456, 1931.
[14]Weekly Article #320, 1929.
[15]Radio Broadcast, April 21, 1935.
[16]Weekly Article #403, 1930.
[17]Weekly Article #196, 1926.
[18]E. R. Squibb & Sons Broadcast, April 20, 1930.
[19]Weekly Article #140, 1925.
[20]Weekly Article #278, 1928.
[21]Weekly Article #535, 1933.

[22]Weekly Article #4, 1932.
[23]New York Times, June 13, 1928.
[24]Daily Telegram, February 27, 1931.
[25]Daily Telegram, September 25, 1932.
[26]Daily Telegram, November 10, 1929.
[27]Radio Broadcast, May 12, 1935.
[28]Daily Telegram, November 1, 1929.
[29]Radio Broadcast, Good Gulf Show, April 30, 1933.
[30]Weekly Article #345, 1929.
[31]Paula McSpadden Love, *The Will Rogers Book,* Michel Mok, newspaper story, 1935, Texian Press, p. 93.
[32]William R. Brown, Imagemaker: *Will Rogers and the American Dream,* University of Missouri Press. p. 18.
[33]Weekly Article #100, 1924.
[34]Weekly Article #513, 1932.
[35]E. R. Squibb & Sons Broadcast, June 1, 1930.
[36]Weekly Article #352, 1929.
[37]Weekly Article #313, 1928.
[38]Weekly Article #218, 1927.
[39]Weekly Article #26, 1923.
[40]Weekly Article #101, 1929.
[41]E. R. Squibb & Sons Broadcast, April 20, 1930.
[42]Weekly Article #491, 1932.
[43]Daily Telegram, April 1, 1935.
[44]Daily Telegram, April 2, 1935.
[45]Daily Telegram, April 28, 1935.
[46]Radio Broadcast, Good Gulf Show, April 30, 1933.
[47]Weekly Article #352, 1929.
[48]Weekly Article #119, 1925.
[49]Weekly Article #26, 1923.
[50]Daily Telegram, February 18, 1929.
[51]Richard M. Ketchum, *Will Rogers -The Man & His Times,* Simon & Schuster, p. 198
[52]Weekly Article # 57, 1924.

Chapter 11, "...As Long As Grass Grows and Water Flows"

[1]E. R. Squibb & Sons Broadcast, April 27, 1930.
[2]David Randolph Milsten, *Will Rogers – The Cherokee Kid,* Glenheath Publishers, p. 51.
[3]Bryan B. & Frances N. Sterling, *Will Rogers in Hollywood,* Crown Publishers, p. 150.
[4]Weekly Article #230, 1927.
[5]Joseph H. Carter, *Never Met a Man I Didn't Like,* Avon Books, p. 15
[6]E. R. Squibb & Sons Broadcast, April 27, 1930.
[7]Radio Broadcast, Good Gulf Show, April 7, 1935.
[8]Radio Broadcast, Good Gulf Show, April 14, 1935.
[9]Radio Broadcast, Good Gulf Show, April 14, 1935.
[10]Weekly Article #486, 1932.
[11]*Saturday Evening Post,* June 2, 1928.

Chapter 12, So-Called Progress

[1]Weekly Article #107, 1924.
[2]Weekly Article #653, 1935.
[3]Weekly Article #151, 1925.
[4]Richard M. Ketchum, *Will Rogers – The Man and His Times,* Simon and Schuster, p. 342 – 343.
[5]Daily Telegram, October 8,1928.
[6]Weekly Article #129, 1925.
[7]Weekly Article #173, 1926.

[8]Will Rogers, *There's Not a Bathing Suit in Russia*, CD-ROM *Presenting Will Rogers*, Will Rogers Memorial, Claremore, Oklahoma.
[9]Weekly Article #173, 1926.
[10]Daily Telegram, December 28, 1932.
[11]Weekly Article #173, 1926.
[12]"How To Be Funny," *American Magazine*, December 1929.
[13]Weekly Article #173, 1926.
[14]E. R. Squibb & Sons Broadcast, June 1, 1930.
[15]Daily Telegram, July 30, 1929.
[16]Weekly Article #226, 1927.

Chapter 13, Civilization–Pro and Con

[1]Weekly Article #530, 1933.
[2]Weekly Article #90, 1924.
[3]Weekly Article #524, 1923.
[4]Weekly Article #353, 1929.
[5]Weekly Article #436, 1931.
[6]Weekly Article #242, 1927.
[7]Weekly Article #169, 1926.
[8]Paula McSpadden Love, *The Will Rogers Book*, Texian Press, p. 146.
[9]Weekly Article #647, 1935.
[10]Weekly Article #445, 1931.
[11]Weekly Article #108, 1925.
[12]Weekly Article #176, 1926.
[13]Weekly Article #385, 1930.
[14]*Saturday Evening Post*, March 30, 1929.
[15]Weekly Article #315, 1929.
[16]Weekly Article #507, 1932.
[17]Weekly Article #112, 1925.
[18]Daily Telegram, September 19, 1932.
[19]Weekly Article #296, 1928.
[20]Weekly Article #353, 1929.
[21]Daily Telegram, November 30, 1932.
[22]Weekly Article #510, 1932.
[23]Weekly Article #147, 1925.
*final statement composed by author to close speech in the spirit of Will Rogers.
[25]Used to open hundreds of speeches and newspaper articles
[26]Weekly Article #630, 1935.
[27]Weekly Article #377, 1930.
[28]Weekly Article #630, 1935.
[29]Weekly Article #388, 1930.
[30]Weekly Article #367, 1930.
[31]Weekly Article #630, 1935.
[32]Weekly Article #49, 1923.
[33]Weekly Article #524, 1933.
[34]Weekly Article #128, 1925.
[35]Weekly Article #342, 1929.
[36]Weekly Article #641, 1935.
[37]Weekly Article #58, 1924.
[38]Weekly Article #136, 1925.
[39]Weekly Article #136, 1925.
[40]Daily Telegram, February 3, 1932.
[41]Weekly Article #13, 1923.
[42]Weekly Article #524, 1933.
[43]David Randolph Milsten, *Will Rogers The Cherokee Kid*, Glenheath Publishers, p. 155.
[44]Weekly Article #445, 1931.

[45]Dale Dauten, *Chicago Tribune*, August 7, 1995.
[46]Radio Broadcast, Good Gulf Show, April 21, 1935.

Chapter 14, What Would Will Have to Say About...?

[1]Daily Telegram, October 27, 1929.
[2]Weekly Article #345, 1929.
[3]Daily Telegram, October 9, 1930.
[4]*Saturday Evening Post*, August 21, 1926.
[5]Weekly Article #1367, 1930.
[6]Weekly Article #454, 1931.
[7]Weekly Article #110, 1925.
[8]Margaret Axtell, *Will Rogers Rode the Range*, The Beatitudes, p. 63.
[9]Daily Telegram, July 9, 1930.
[10]Daily Telegram, April 28, 1930.
[11]Weekly Article #363, 1929.
[12]Weekly Article #540, 1933.
[13]Weekly Article #36, 1923.
[14]Weekly Article #59, 1924.
[15]Daily Telegram, July 4, 1930.
[16]Weekly Article #3, 1922.
[17]Weekly Article #278, 1928.
[18]Weekly Article #91, 1924.
[19]Weekly Article #128, 1925.
[20]Weekly Article #128, 1925.
[21]Weekly Article #103, 1924.
[22]Weekly Article #319, 1929.
[23]Daily Telegram, May 15, 1928.
[24]Daily Telegram, October 30, 1932.
[25]Daily Telegram, May 11, 1934.
[26]Daily Telegram, September 10, 1934.
[27]Weekly Article #115, 1925.
[28]*Saturday Evening Post*, August 28, 1926.
[29]Weekly Article #461, 1931.
[30]Weekly Article #158, 1925.
[31]Daily Telegram, October 30, 1927.
[32]Weekly Article #88, 1924.
[33]Daily Telegram, June 15, 1930.
[34]Weekly Article #541, 1933.
[35]*Saturday Evening Post*, July 31, 1926.
[36]Readers Digest, December 11, 1989.
[37]Daily Telegram, August 16, 1934.
[38]Weekly Article #340, 1929.
[39]Weekly Article #107, 1924.
[40]Weekly Article #548, 1933.
[41]Daily Telegram, March 16, 1932.
[42]Weekly Article #8, 1923.
[43]Bryan B. Sterling, *The Will Rogers Scrapbook*, Crown Publishers, Inc. p. 7.
[44]Weekly Article #347, 1929.
[45]Weekly Article #378, 1930.
[46]E. R. Squibb & Sons Broadcast, May 11, 1930.
[47]Weekly Article #278, 1928.
[48]Weekly Article #129, 1925.
[49]Daily Telegram, February 13, 1930.
[50]Daily Telegram, April 19, 1929.
[51]Daily Telegram, May 29, 1930.
[52]Daily Telegram, June 19, 1935.

[53]Weekly Article #315, 1929.
[54]Weekly Article #21, 1923.
[55]Daily Telegram, July 7, 1930.
[56]Joseph H. Carter, *Never Met a Man I Didn't Like*, Avon Books, p. 272.
[57]Weekly Article #379, 1930.
[58]Daily Telegram, December. 9, 1930.
[59]Daily Telegram, March 27, 1932.
[60]Weekly Article #78, 1924.
[61]Daily Telegram, June 5, 1931.
[62]Daily Telegram, November 28, 1934.
[63]Weekly Article #50, 1923.
[64]Weekly Article #56, 1924.
[65]Daily Telegram, February 1, 1933.
[66]Weekly Article #518, 1932.
[67]Daily Telegram, April 30, 1929.
[68]Weekly Article #360, 1929.
[69]Weekly Article #397, 1930.
[70]Radio Broadcast, Good Gulf Show, May 5, 1935.
[71]Weekly Article #56, 1924
[72]Daily Telegram, February 1, 1935.
[73]Will Rogers Memorial Archives Scrap Book 8-1 p. 44.
[74]Weekly Article #143, 1925.
[75]Daily Telegram, April 23, 1933.
[76]Weekly Article #327, 1929.
[77]Daily Telegram, May 23, 1932.

Chapter 15, Heroes and Hope

[1]Daily Telegram, July 17, 1928.
[2]Weekly Article #644, 1935.
[3]Weekly Article #559, 1933.
[4]Parade Magazine, *Chicago Tribune*, August 6, 1995.
[5]Weekly Article #115, 1925.
[6]Weekly Article #115, 1925.
[7]Weekly Article #305, 1928.
[8]Weekly Article #411, 1930.
[9]Weekly Article #411, 1930.

When you are in Oklahoma, be sure to visit the Will Rogers Memorial and Birthplace.

Will Rogers Memorial – In 1938, the Rogers family donated a twenty-acre site in Claremore, Oklahoma, where the state built a towering Memorial. In 1944, the bodies of Will and Betty Rogers were interred there along with family members. Over a half century, the Memorial was expanded and enhanced to include theaters, interactive exhibits, and eight galleries of art and artifacts. The museum attracts millions of visitors. Archives and a library were established and are actively maintained.

Will Rogers Birthplace – The original birthplace house near Oologah, Oklahoma, was carefully preserved on the original Rogers ranch. A half century after Will Rogers' death, it has become an "1879 living history ranch" open to tourists, with Texas Longhorn cattle, other farm animals, and outbuildings.

For further information on the Memorial and Birthplace write:

Will Rogers Memorial and Birthplace
P.O. Box #157
Claremore, Oklahoma 74018-0157

or call: (918) 341-0719.